Due Dec 20,02

Great Medical Discoveries

Reproductive Technology

Other books in the Great Medical Discoveries series:

Anesthetics
Chemotherapy
Cloning
Gene Therapy
Germs
Heart Transplants
The Microscope
Tuberculosis
Vaccines

Great Medical Discoveries

Reproductive Technology

by Kim K. Zach

LUCENT
BOOKS®

THOMSON
*
GALE

San Diego • Detroit • New York • San Francisco • Cleveland • New Haven, Conn. • Waterville, Maine • London • Munich

LIBRARY OF CONGRESS CATALOGING-IN-PUBLICATION DATA

Zach, Kim K., 1958–
  Reproductive technology / by Kim K. Zach.
    v. cm. — (Great medical discoveries)
Includes bibliographical references and index.
Contents: Treating male infertility: artificial and donor insemination—The keystone of
assisted reproduction: in vitro fertilization—Surrogacy, egg donation, and embryo adoption—Preventing inherited disease: preimplantation genetic diagnosis—Drawing the
line: ethical, moral, and social questions.
  ISBN 1-59018-344-4 (hardback : alk. paper)
  1. Human reproductive technology—Juvenile literature. [1. Human reproductive
technology.] I. Title. II. Series.
  RG133.5.Z33 2004
  618.1'78—dc22
                                     2003015403

CONTENTS

FOREWORD

Throughout history, people have struggled to understand and conquer the diseases and physical ailments that plague us. Once in a while, a discovery has changed the course of medicine and sometimes, the course of history itself. The stories of these discoveries have many elements in common—accidental findings, sudden insights, human dedication, and most of all, powerful results. Many illnesses that in the past were essentially a death warrant for their sufferers are today curable or even virtually extinct. And exciting new directions in medicine promise a future in which the building blocks of human life itself—the genes—may be manipulated and altered to restore health or to prevent disease from occurring in the first place.

It has been said that an insight is simply a re-arrangement of already-known facts, and as often as not, these great medical discoveries have resulted partly from a reexamination of earlier efforts in light of new knowledge. Nineteenth-century monk Gregor Mendel experimented with pea plants for years, quietly unlocking the mysteries of genetics. However, the importance of his findings went unnoticed until three separate scientists, studying cell division with a newly improved invention called a microscope, rediscovered his work decades after his death. French doctor Jean-Antoine Villemin's experiments with rabbits proved that tuberculosis was contagious, but his conclusions were politely ignored by the medical community until another doctor, Robert Koch of Germany, discovered the exact culprit—the tubercle bacillus germ—years later.

Accident, too, has played a part in some medical discoveries. Because the tuberculosis germ does not stain with dye as easily as other bacteria, Koch was able to see it only after he had let a treated slide sit far longer than he intended. An unwanted speck of mold led Englishman Alexander Fleming to recognize the bacteria-killing qualities of the penicillium fungi, ushering in the era of antibiotic "miracle drugs."

That researchers sometimes benefited from fortuitous accidents does not mean that they were bumbling amateurs who relied solely on luck. They were dedicated scientists whose work created the conditions under which such lucky events could occur; many sacrificed years of their lives to observation and experimentation. Sometimes the price they paid was higher. Rene Launnec, who invented the stethoscope to help him study the effects of tuberculosis, himself succumbed to the disease.

And humanity has benefited from these scientists' efforts. The formerly terrifying disease of smallpox has been eliminated from the face of the earth—the only case of the complete conquest of a once deadly disease. Tuberculosis, perhaps the oldest disease known to humans and certainly one of its most prolific killers, has been essentially wiped out in some parts of the world. Genetically engineered insulin is a godsend to countless diabetics who are allergic to the animal insulin that has traditionally been used to help them.

Despite such triumphs there are few unequivocal success stories in the history of great medical discoveries. New strains of tuberculosis are proving to be resistant to the antibiotics originally developed to treat them, raising the specter of a resurgence of the disease that has killed 2 billion people over the course of human history. But medical research continues on numerous fronts and will no doubt lead to still undreamed-of advancements in the future.

Each volume in the Great Medical Discoveries series tells the story of one great medical breakthrough—the first gropings for understanding, the pieces that came together and how, and the immediate and longer-term results. Part science and part social history, the series explains some of the key findings that have shaped modern medicine and relieved untold human suffering. Numerous primary and secondary source quotations enhance the text and bring to life all the drama of scientific discovery. Sidebars highlight personalities and convey personal stories. The series also discusses the future of each medical discovery—a future in which vaccines may guard against AIDS, gene therapy may eliminate cancer, and other as-yet unimagined treatments may become commonplace.

INTRODUCTION

Reproductive Technology: New Hope for Infertile Couples

Infertility is not a new problem. Couples throughout history have experienced the physical and emotional pain of being unable to have a child. Little help was available, largely due to a lack of knowledge about the human body and the reproductive system. For many, the only sources of information were myths and old wives' tales. Thus, couples wanting children turned to folk remedies and magic potions. Not surprisingly, they met with limited success. For centuries the only options for infertile couples were to remain childless, ask someone else to bear a child for them, or—if the man was sterile—find another man to father a child.

The first significant development in reproductive medicine was artificial insemination—that is, introducing a man's sperm into a woman without having sexual intercourse—although early experiments in humans did not begin until the late 1800s, and even then it was a simplistic procedure at best. As scientists began to uncover and understand the intricate details of conception and birth, the technical application of that knowledge lagged far behind. Medical intervention was necessary in order to overcome the physical causes of infertility, but doctors did not yet have the methods or means to undertake that intervention successfully.

Once scientists developed hormone regimens for women that could stimulate ovulation, and surgical techniques that could retrieve ripened eggs, a variety of treatments became possible. Yet even as recently as the 1960s and 1970s, the medical procedures that would form the core of reproductive technology were merely the stuff of science-fiction novels. In the last few decades of the twentieth century, the field of reproductive technology has exploded, offering new hope to the estimated 6 million couples in the United States—one in every ten—who suffer from infertility.

In recent decades, advances in reproductive technology have helped millions of infertile couples to conceive children.

Defining Infertility

Infertility can be one of two types. Primary infertility is defined as the inability to conceive a child after one year of unprotected intercourse. It also includes the inability to maintain a pregnancy to term. Sometimes following the birth of their first baby a couple has difficulty achieving a second pregnancy. This inability to conceive again is known as secondary infertility. Both types of infertility are equally common.

Infertility was traditionally viewed as a woman's problem. Childless women were known as barren and often were cast aside by their husbands for failing to produce offspring. However, scientific evidence holds that infertility can be equally attributed to men and women. About 40 percent of couples will be told their infertility is due to a female factor; another 40 percent will have their problems attributed to the man. Twenty percent of the time, the problem is due to a combination of male and female factors or the infertility remains unexplained.

Whatever the reason, infertility can sometimes strain a relationship. "Although specialists are careful not to use language that suggests 'fault' or 'blame,'" says author and attorney Lynda Beck Fenwick, "most infertile couples struggle to avoid those feelings completely. Statistically, male factors are involved nearly as frequently as female factors, and so, both husbands and wives know the guilt of being unable to accomplish their part in the reproductive process, and both husbands and wives know the resentment of being the fertile partner in an infertile marriage."[1]

A Growing Dilemma

The number of infertile couples in the United States has risen steadily since 1965, and experts predict that infertility will continue to increase. They believe a variety of social factors—such as delayed childbearing, sexually transmitted diseases (STDs), and lifestyle choices—are responsible for the increase.

Among women throughout much of the world, the single most important element in the rising infertility rate is a marked increase in the age at which they begin trying to have children. Statistics show that women in the age group thirty-five to forty-four have the most difficulty conceiving. A woman's fertility is at its peak when she is in her twenties, declines through her thirties, and drops dramatically after age forty. Yet, for financial and career reasons, women are waiting longer to start their families. Ironically, just as a working woman may begin to think about having a baby, her ability to conceive has been compromised by her age.

An epidemic of STDs has also affected the fertility of both men and women. Millions of cases are diagnosed each year, but some STDs produce no symptoms. If left untreated, these infections can damage or block a woman's fallopian tubes, making it impossible for an egg to be fertilized. In men, scarring may occur in the urethra, thus blocking the passage of sperm.

Use of cigarettes, alcohol, and drugs are all known to impair fertility by reducing the production of, or by causing abnormilities in, the eggs and sperm. Use of these substances may also disrupt the production or action of hormones that regulate reproductive cycles. Other lifestyle factors of modern-day living that are known to affect fertility are exercise, diet, stress, and environmental and workplace hazards.

Infertility Treatments

Whatever the explanation for the increase in infertility, the progressive development of reproductive technologies during the twentieth century has been a boon for infertile couples. With each new decade, the array of options has expanded, offering help for problems previously considered insurmountable. For example, artificial insemination and donor insemination (DI), which might overcome problems with sperm production, were of little use for women who did not ovulate or who had blocked fallopian tubes. However, these conditions became treatable when hormone drug therapy and microsurgery techniques were developed.

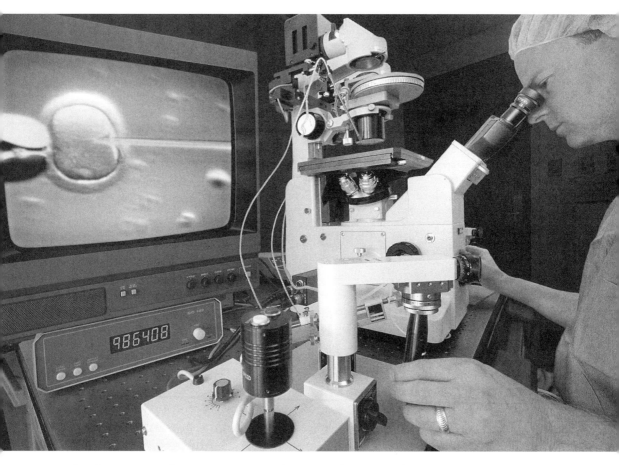

In the twenty-five years since the introduction of in vitro fertilization (IVF) there are more treatments available than ever before. The IVF procedure, which involves fertilization of an egg outside a woman's body then placing the egg in the woman's uterus, has generated a wide variety of more complex and more invasive forms of high-tech conception. These IVF-related procedures have opened a host of possibilities for couples with many types of fertility problems. In fact, more than one hundred thousand children have been conceived and born through IVF or related technology.

A technician uses a microscope to inject sperm into an egg. This procedure was developed to assist couples undergoing in vitro fertilization.

Limits of Scientific Knowledge

At the same time, reproductive technology has raised many ethical, social, and legal questions. Gina Kolata, author of *Clone: The Road to Dolly and the Path Ahead*, says that this area, though, is often overlooked. She writes,

> At first the feats of reproductive scientists were the objects of controversy and shock. But we have become accustomed to their achievements. And it is hard to argue against the cries that couples have a right to reproductive freedom. Many have suffered for years, yearning for a child of their own. If they want to create babies, and are paying with their own money, who has the right to tell them no?[2]

However, because advances in technology occur at such a rapid pace, a new procedure is often implemented long before its effects can be completely studied. Thus, infertile patients can be helped in the short term, but the full implications cannot be known immediately. For example, does taking fertility drugs increase the risk of ovarian cancer? Are IVF babies more likely to be born with genetic defects? What are the long-term effects on children born from frozen eggs or embryos?

Despite these questions, most experts believe that the push to use the new technology will continue. For most infertile couples, the desire to have a child is the most powerful force operating in their lives. Most are willing to risk nearly anything—time, money, sorrow, and pain— in order to conceive a child. Reproductive technology offers them hope that couples in past centuries did not have.

Brian Kearney, author of *High-Tech Conception: A Comprehensive Handbook for Consumers*, explains:

> Assisted reproduction in the United States has become a multi-billion dollar industry that sells hope—hope that a diagnosis of infertility is not a life sentence of childlessness. Each month brings a new discovery, a new approach, a new reason to keep on trying. And for the thousands who have been successful, assisted reproduction has brought a source of incredible joy: the children they had wanted for so long but dared not believe would ever be born.[3]

CHAPTER 1

Treating Male Infertility: Artificial and Donor Insemination

W hen a fertility specialist attempts to aid a couple in becoming parents, one of the first reproductive technologies turned to involves shortening the trip sperm normally must take en route to the egg. Artificial insemination accomplishes this by positioning sperm as close to the fallopian tubes as possible. There, if the timing is right, a ripened egg should be waiting.

A Long History

The concept of artificial insemination—that is, the introduction of sperm into a woman's body by means other than sexual intercourse—has a long history, although its widespread use in humans is fairly recent. Not until the latter half of the twentieth century, when new preservation techniques allowed sperm to be stored for later use and procedures for determining when a woman's fertility was at its peak were developed, did artificial insemination become a widely used and highly reliable means of assisting human reproduction.

Early Ideas About the Role of Sperm

As early as the third century A.D., scholars debated the possibility of human insemination by artificial means, even though scientists of the day had no knowledge of the intricacies of conception. While they did realize that semen was in some way connected to the process, they had no way of knowing that a drop of semen held millions of individual sperm cells.

Even after the invention of the microscope in the 1600s, which enabled scientists to view sperm cells for the first time, misunderstandings about the role of sperm in achieving pregnancy prevailed. According to a popular theory of the time (known today as preformationism), within each sperm cell was the body of a human infant, minute but complete. People believed that during the period of gestation in the womb, this tiny creature simply grew larger until it was ready to be born.

Preformationism fit nicely with another notion of the day: that when a couple was childless, it was never the man's fault. People were led to believe, as Susan Lewis Cooper and Ellen Sarasohn Glazer, authors of *Choosing Assisted Reproduction* and experts in the social and emotional aspects of infertility, explain:

> The man plants the seed of his future child in much the same way that a farmer plants seeds in the ground. If the soil is not fertile, the land will be barren. Thus, it is easy to understand why our ancestors believed that women alone were responsible for infertility. Since sperm could not be seen in an ejaculate—let alone be counted, as they are today—our ancestors must have assumed that if a man ejaculated his seed, he was fertile.[4]

Artificial Insemination of Animals

Whatever people believed regarding the nature of sperm and its role in conception, they did attempt to put artificial insemination to practical use. Accounts from the 1400s, for example, tell of Arabian horse breeders seeking to use artificial insemination to improve the bloodlines of their herds. Several centuries later, Lazzaro

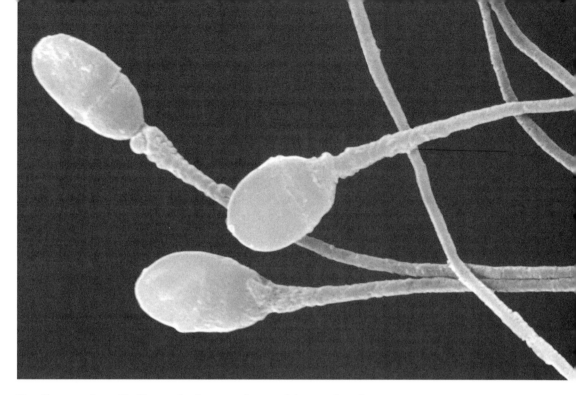

Spallanzani, an Italian scholar, performed insemination experiments with reptiles and dogs as his subjects. In one experiment in 1782 a female spaniel gave birth to three puppies she conceived through artificial insemination. Sometimes called the father of artificial insemination because of his studies, Spallanzani proved for the first time that sperm and egg must meet in order for an embryo to develop.

Early scientists mistakenly believed that sperm cells were tiny human bodies waiting to grow. Today, scientists understand the true nature and function of sperm.

Only a few years later, London physician John Hunter recorded the birth of the first human conceived through artificial insemination. Hunter's patient was a woman whose husband was able to produce sperm, but because of a physical abnormality, the discharge of sperm was blocked. Although the conception was considered a major medical breakthrough at the time, it was not a particularly sophisticated procedure, at least by modern standards. Science writer Gina Maranto says:

> At its simplest, artificial insemination barely qualifies as a technology. No complicated instruments, drugs, or physiological calculations are involved, merely the collection of sperm and insertion of them. . . . Certainly the early attempts by [Hunter] and others required little more than a syringe and a sense of timing. [5]

Throughout the 1800s and early 1900s, physicians in Europe and the United States continued to treat infertility by inseminating women with their husband's sperm. However, possibly because of concerns that the procedure ran counter to widely held religious values, few records of these attempts were kept.

"Only a handful of case studies of artificial insemination surfaced in the medical literature from the turn of the century through 1940," explains Maranto:

> Accordingly, it is almost impossible to document how many women underwent the procedure . . . during this period. In 1924, one researcher, having made a concerted effort to track down every citation in the literature, tallied 123 artificial inseminations, of which 47 led to pregnancy. A separate study carried out four years later located evidence of 185 attempts worldwide, with 65 pregnancies ensuing. These assessments apparently jibed with the medical community's anecdotal sense of the procedure's prevalence.[6]

Sperm cells swim toward an egg. Only one sperm cell will be able to fertilize the egg and begin the reproductive process.

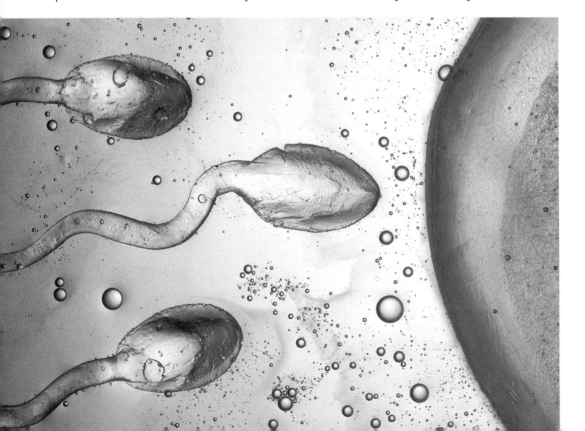

The Concept of Donor Insemination (DI)

While doctors knew that artificial insemination could result in pregnancy, it was no help for couples if the husband was incapable of producing sperm. The only solution in such cases was to use someone else's—a donor's—sperm. Yet, if artificial insemination using a husband's sperm raised objections on religious grounds, even more objectionable was the use of donor sperm. This element added to the secrecy surrounding artificial insemination as physicians surreptitiously continued to help their patients achieve pregnancy.

In 1884 the first known successful artificial insemination using donor sperm occurred at Jefferson Medical College in Philadelphia, Pennsylvania. Physician William Pancoast used sperm provided by a medical student at the college to inseminate a patient whose husband, tests had shown, was sterile. Pancoast performed the insemination on the pretext of giving his patient an examination; he told no one, not even his patient or her husband, about the use of donated sperm until after the birth of the baby, a boy. At this point he told the husband, who was surprisingly accepting of the news. The husband simply asked that Pancoast keep the facts behind their son's conception a secret from his wife. After Pancoast died in 1909, however, one of the students present at the procedure revealed what he knew in a medical journal.

A public outpouring of letters, both for and against artificial insemination, followed this revelation. Those who approved of Pancoast's actions cited the obvious benefits to childless couples. Some critics accused Pancoast of immoral behavior, but supporters responded that morality was the concern of religious leaders, not scientists. Still other critics expressed the fear that husbands would no longer be a necessary part of the reproductive process. So, even at the dawn of reproductive technology, battle lines were being drawn. As Maranto explains, "Without forethought or intention, Pancoast helped launch the age of assisted reproduction, ushering in a host of ethical, legal, and social concerns which even today remain largely unresolved."[7]

Resistance to DI

During the first half of the twentieth century, the use of DI grew more common but failed to reach its potential for helping large numbers of infertile couples. For one thing, many men rejected the idea of having a child who was not genetically related to them—a child who some felt represented their failure as men. Complicating matters was the legal status of children conceived by DI. Biologist and geneticist Lee M. Silver writes, "Some legislatures and courts in the United States, Canada, and England equated DI with adultery and DI children were labeled illegitimate, even if the husband consented to the procedure . . . [this attitude] . . . held sway into the 1960s."[8]

In 1964 Georgia became the first state to pass a law making children conceived by DI legitimate if husband and wife both provided written consent. A decade later, the American Bar Association and the National Conference of Commissioners on Uniform State Laws approved the Uniform Parentage Act and recommended that states adopt it into law. Nineteen states went on to adopt the act, and several others enacted portions of it.

In states that adopted the model law, one portion of the act made clear the legal status of any man whose wife was artificially inseminated with donor sperm with her husband's consent while under the care of a doctor. The statute clearly stated that the husband, not the donor, was the legal father. The act also specifically banned the use of the term "illegitimate" to describe children conceived in this way.

In spite of these legal clarifications, various faiths held fast to their objections to DI on moral grounds. For example, the Roman Catholic Church held that sex, love, and procreation should not be separated. The church held, therefore, that any child born of such artificial means

Assessing Male Fertility

When a couple seeks medical help for suspected infertility, the husband is usually tested first. Sperm analysis, the fundamental test for men, is an uncomplicated procedure. Once a semen sample is obtained, it is then analyzed for one or more deficiencies that could cause the infertility. One such deficiency is low sperm count (*oligospermia*). Sperm count is calculated by the number of sperm per milliliter of ejaculate. A good sperm count is 20 million per milliliter. Fewer than 10 million can impair fertility, and below 1 million is considered severely infertile. Other problems include poor sperm motility (*asthenospermia*), which is the sperms' ability to swim and propel themselves forward quickly, or poor sperm morphology (*teratospermia*), referring to sperm structure. Examples of poor morphology include sperm with deformed tails, two heads, no tails, or no heads. Sometimes no sperm is present in a man's semen, a condition known as *azoospermia*.

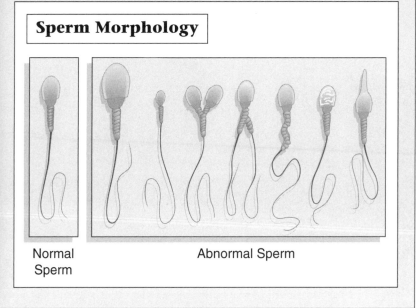

Sperm Morphology

Normal Sperm

Abnormal Sperm

was morally illegitimate. As a consequence of such continued religious disapproval, DI continued to be performed under a cloud of secrecy. Physicians, moreover, routinely advised couples not to tell their children the circumstances of their conception.

Problems with Storing Sperm

In addition to religious opposition, there was another problem with using donated sperm: Unless the donor could make himself available at the precise moment when a woman's egg was ready to be fertilized, the sperm's short shelf life made the procedure impractical. Some means of preserving sperm was needed.

The means scientists hit upon was cryopreservation, which literally means "to save by freezing." Scientists already knew that some types of tissue could be preserved by freezing. The trick with sperm was to keep from killing the cells they were trying to preserve and have them able to actually fertilize an egg once they were thawed.

Spallanzani had been the first to observe that when sperm were cooled (he used snow) they became motionless; upon being warmed, they began to move again. Actually freezing sperm, however, was another matter. Around 1866 another Italian, a physician named Paolo

Freezing and Storing Sperm for Later Insemination

After a fresh semen specimen is collected in a sterile container, a small amount (about one-tenth the volume of the sample) of glycerol is added, and the two substances are thoroughly combined. Then the mixture is siphoned into a plastic straw, frozen by exposure to liquid nitrogen vapors, and submerged into the liquid nitrogen for storage. When the frozen sperm is needed for insemination, the straw is taken out of the nitrogen and thawed at room temperature, or briefly in warm water. A syringe or catheter is used to place the sperm directly into the woman's body. The closer the sperm can be placed to the egg, the more likely the egg will be fertilized.

Sperm cells are frozen for artificial insemination.

Mantegazza, managed to cool frog sperm to minus five degrees Fahrenheit without any apparent negative consequences. Mantegazza envisioned the banking of frozen human sperm for later use. He even composed a tale about a soldier dying in battle but whose wife was later inseminated with sperm he had left behind.

Bridging the gap between fantasy and reality took nearly another century. Scientists were able to freeze sperm, but for reasons that remained unclear, many sperm did not survive. During the 1930s, researchers experimented with both freezing and thawing procedures. For example, they varied the speed at which sperm were frozen, quickly submerging samples in below-freezing solutions or gradually cooling them until they were frozen. Similarly they varied the speed of thawing the sperm—sometimes rapidly, other times slowly. No matter what researchers did, however, approximately half the sperm died. Worse, scientists could not be sure whether the surviving sperm were viable—that is, capable of fertilizing an egg.

During this time, Basile Luyet, a French-born scientist working in the United States, concluded that ice crystals within the cells were the problem with most types of tissue. Ice normally caused irreparable damage to cells. Paradoxically, some means of freezing was needed that would not result in the formation of ice crystals.

In 1945 British scientist Alan Parkes speculated that the manner of storage was more important than the speed of freezing and thawing. Parkes was convinced that whereas scientists had been freezing sperm in thin layers or in small tubes, larger tubes would improve the number of surviving sperm, and he was correct. He then directed his focus toward developing a more sperm-friendly liquid solution for added protection for the sperm while stored in the tubes. In 1949, in a lab mix-up, one of Parkes's assistants added 5 percent glycerol into the solution, and this proved to be the perfect insulator for the sperm. Glycerol, a slippery, colorless liquid, protected the sperm from injury during freezing because it replaced water inside the cells, thus greatly reducing the formation of ice crystals.

In 1953 American doctor Jerome K. Sherman, using the glycerol solution, slow-cooled sperm and stored them using dry ice as the refrigerant. This method allowed more than 70 percent of the sperm to survive. Shortly after, Sherman reported the birth to a woman in Iowa City, Iowa, of the first baby conceived with frozen sperm. A number of other researchers attempted to copy the feat. Maranto writes, "fifteen other such births took place over the next five years [and] . . . "

> Japanese physicians boldly adopted the use of frozen sperm, and reported two dozen pregnancies by 1965. However, not all of these went to term, and at least one baby was stillborn. Just eight years later, five hundred babies had been delivered worldwide thanks to frozen sperm, and medical investigators had satisfied themselves that the technique was safe and produced rates of anomaly no worse than natural conception. [9]

Banking Frozen Sperm

Sherman, however, had more ambitious goals than simply improving cryopreservation techniques. In 1963 in a speech before his fellow scientists at the eleventh International Congress of Human Genetics, Sherman shared his vision for the development of sperm banks. At the time, Sherman's vision of a future for sperm banks attracted little attention from the general public. In 1969, for example, a poll showed that only 3 percent of Americans had ever even heard of artificial insemination. That lack of awareness, however, gradually changed as the first sperm banks began operation.

In the early 1970s, the focus of sperm banks was largely to provide a service to men who were planning to have a vasectomy or who faced medical treatments, such as those for cancer, that could cause sterility. Sperm banking allowed these men to store healthy sperm in case they wanted to be fathers in the future. In the years that followed, men who worked with chemicals known to reduce fertility or cause genetic defects would also become interested in storing their sperm as fertility insurance.

Cryopreservation helped expand the use of artificial insemination and made possible the use of sperm banks. Still, a 1979 University of Wisconsin study uncovered the fact that although a large number of doctors were quietly using DI to help patients become pregnant, they were using fresh—not frozen—sperm. It turned out that this was because research of the day indicated that, statistically, pregnancy rates were higher with fresh sperm, and doctors were, after all, in the business of helping infertile couples have children.

What changed doctors' attitudes regarding cryopreservation was the discovery of HIV, the organism that causes AIDS. Because the virus can be transmitted through bodily fluids including semen, the possibility existed that recipients of fresh donor sperm ran the risk of being infected. On the other hand, freezing meant that sperm could be donated and the donor monitored for however long it took to be certain he was not HIV-positive. In response to the AIDS threat, different medical organizations began recommending against the use of fresh semen. The American Society for Reproductive Medicine, the U.S. Food and Drug Administration, and the Centers for Disease Control and Prevention all supported the use of frozen semen.

Eventually these groups developed strict guidelines for sperm banks to follow. These guidelines require rigorous donor screening. Potential donors are interviewed to determine their risk factors for HIV infection. They go through a routine physical examination to note any obvious signs of infection and give a blood sample, which is tested for HIV and antibodies to the virus. All of these tests are performed at the time of donation and again six months later. Following the six-month quarantine, if the donor has no sign of HIV, the frozen sperm can be used. Donors are also screened for other STDs, as well as for genetic abnormalities.

Keeping the Secret

As a result of the traditional disapproval of DI, many people are reluctant to discuss the procedure. For example, many physicians fail to address—both before and after treatment—the loss felt by men who raise a child "fathered" by another man. Furthermore, this lack of counseling extends to the sperm donors as well. Cooper and Glazer explain that "although sperm banks are recognizing that donor families have long-term needs that must be addressed and are adapting their services accordingly, they do not seem to be acknowledging that donating sperm—even anonymously—may have ramifications for a man's future."[10]

It is impossible to know for certain how many children have been born through DI. Some experts say the figure could be near 1 million. In scientific terms, this simple reproductive technology has been a success. But some psychologists and other people wonder about the effect DI has had on family dynamics, the children, and the donors.

More sperm banks are now offering an identity-release clause, or openness policy, as part of their regular screening process. If a donor agrees, his identity can be revealed, although many donors may not consider the impact this might later have on their lives, including what to tell a spouse or children they may have in the future. As of 2003, there were no laws in the United States requiring sperm banks to maintain donor records, although that may change. Many reproductive specialists believe that, at the very least, children should have access to their medical and genetic heritage. "The important thing for a child is to be able to visualize the donor," says Annette Baran, an infertility specialist and the coauthor of *Lethal Secrets: The Psychology of Donor Insemination*. "It's not a teaspoon of sperm, it's a person."[11]

A doctor discusses the ramifications of a man's decision to donate sperm to a donor insemination clinic.

Preserving Potential Fertility

Mantegazza's vision of soldiers leaving behind their legacy in the form of frozen sperm came true 150 years after his prediction. Once cryopreservation made the long-term storage and later use of sperm possible, the technology, as so often happens, began to be applied for purposes beyond its original intended use—that is, infertility. During the 1992 Persian Gulf War, for example, a

Sperm Retrieval After Death

Technology now exists that allows physicians to collect sperm after a man has died and to freeze it. Two such techniques are microsurgical epididymal sperm aspiration (MESA) and testicular sperm extraction (TSE). According to the University of Pennsylvania Center for Bioethics, clinics in several states have retrieved sperm from deceased males. For many women, the loss of a partner has been less devastating because they have been given the option of bearing his child following his death.

number of servicemen chose to bank their sperm before they were deployed to the Middle East as genetic insurance in the event they were killed. Leading U.S. sperm banks are reporting an increase in the number of requests for their services by GIs heading overseas.

Freezing sperm has also become a regular occurrence for men undergoing radiation or chemotherapy. In the event their cancer treatment leaves them sterile or somehow damages their ability to produce healthy sperm, their previously frozen sperm allows them the chance of fathering children.

While many couples find the answer to their infertility problems in artificial or donor insemination, it is not the appropriate treatment in some cases. For example, women with irregular ovulation or tubal blockages will require more complex medical intervention, as will men with a low sperm count or blocked ducts. Recent developments in hormone drug therapies and microsurgery techniques have allowed specialists to extend the range of help to include these causes of infertility.

CHAPTER 2

Fertility Enhancement: Drug Therapy and Microsurgery

Artificial insemination is generally simpler, less expensive, and less invasive than other types of reproductive technology. However, it cannot help all infertile couples. For example, if a woman's fallopian tubes are blocked, artificial insemination will be of no use because the sperm will have no way of reaching the egg. In other instances, a woman may experience some sort of irregularity in her egg-producing cycle, or a man may have a low sperm count for physical reasons. These sorts of problems cannot be treated with artificial insemination. But with the development of ovulation-stimulating drugs and advances in microsurgery techniques, such infertile couples were given two other options. They could embark upon a course of hormone treatment to boost sperm or egg production or, when appropriate, undergo surgical procedures to correct structural abnormalities.

Female Hormone Imbalance

In about one-third of the cases of female infertility, a hormonal problem of some kind is the culprit. Normal egg production, or ovulation, depends on a series of key hormones being produced at the right time and in the right amounts. The ovulation process is complex and occasionally, as with any complicated process, something goes wrong. When that happens, infertility is frequently the result. Correcting the problem, then, involves supplementing the body's normal hormone production, either with naturally occurring hormones or with similar, artificially synthesized, substances.

Understanding the Role of Hormones

Before the early 1900s hormones had not even been named, nor their role in fertility identified. Still, some scientists suspected that something controlled various bodily functions, including a woman's monthly menstrual cycle. In the late 1800s, Walter Heape, a noted biologist at Cambridge University in the United Kingdom, was exploring the interrelated processes of ovulation, fertilization, and gestation. Conducted largely with rabbits, Heape's experiments led him to conclude that some force controlled the regular monthly changes a female rabbit experienced. He eventually formed the notion that a substance circulating through the body prompted the release of an egg from the ovary.

Although Heape was on the right track, he and other scientists of the era were in the dark about the timing of the sequence of events that made up a woman's menstrual cycle. For example, they mistakenly believed that menstruation and ovulation happened at the same time. This misconception would be corrected only after several more decades of research.

Meanwhile, scientists were learning more about the nature of reproductive organs and how they worked. In 1910 F.H.A. Marshall, a Cambridge University lecturer and an admirer of Heape's work, had gathered enough evidence from animal experiments to determine that the

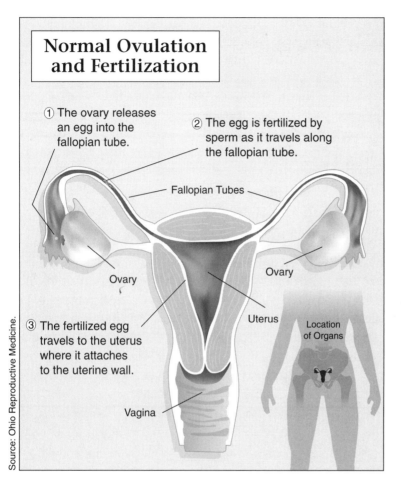

Normal Ovulation and Fertilization

① The ovary releases an egg into the fallopian tube.

② The egg is fertilized by sperm as it travels along the fallopian tube.

Fallopian Tubes

Ovary

Ovary

③ The fertilized egg travels to the uterus where it attaches to the uterine wall.

Uterus

Location of Organs

Vagina

Source: Ohio Reproductive Medicine.

ovaries not only produced eggs in response to hormonal stimulation but were themselves secreters of hormonal substances. He was the first scientist to show a relationship between secretions from the ovaries and changes in the lining of the uterus during the female reproductive cycle.

Marshall's work laid the foundation for future knowledge about the role of internal secretions in the mechanics of reproduction. During the next two decades, the main hormones controlling the woman's reproductive cycle were identified. One the researchers called FSH, for follicle stimulating hormone, since it regulated the growth of the follicles, the structures that release the egg. In addition, they identified the hormone that controls the release of the egg into the fallopian tubes, luteinizing hormone (LH), and the hormone that triggers ovulation, human chorionic gonadotropin (hCG). In 1928 researchers at the University of Rochester in New York identified the hormone progesterone and determined its function, that of preparing the uterus for pregnancy. The next year, Edward Doisy of Washington University in St. Louis, Missouri, isolated and identified the hormone estrogen, which, like progesterone, aids in fertilization and the implantation of the embryo in the uterus.

Controlling Ovulation from the Outside

By the 1940s, scientists understood that hormones control the production of eggs, and keep a pregnancy on track by stopping the production of additional eggs. Two hormones secreted by the ovaries, estrogen and progesterone, are key. Estrogen sends a message to the brain's pituitary gland, which produces FSH and hCG, to stop producing these hormones. Progesterone stops the production of LH. Furthermore, researchers found that they could supplement a woman's natural production of these hormones with injections. This was an important discovery, as it would lead scientists to further explore the therapeutic uses of hormones, such as contraception and fertility treatments. Yet scientists faced a major roadblock to such treatments. Progesterone could only be taken from animal sources, and since it was only produced in small amounts, it was expensive. Huge doses were required, and the injections were painful and difficult for the body to metabolize.

In 1943 Russell Marker, a chemist and professor at Pennsylvania State University in State College, Pennsylvania, devised a method of extracting progesterone from plants; he also discovered a way to make estrogen in his lab. One problem remained: Like natural progesterone from animal sources, the synthetic progesterone required injections of large quantities to be effective.

Developing Fertility Drugs

Ironically, the first application of the synthetic (that is, lab-produced) estrogen, clomiphene citrate, was as a contraceptive, since large doses of estrogen stop ovulation. As expected, when injected into animals, clomiphene citrate stopped production of FSH and LH. But when it was tested in humans, the opposite effect occurred. Instead of preventing ovulation, the drug stimulated follicle growth. Often, multiple eggs would be released. As a result, a drug that was originally thought to be a promising method of birth control became one of the most widely used drugs to boost fertility. Sherman J. Silber, author of *How to Get Pregnant with the New Technology*, comments:

> Many great biological discoveries are sheer accidents, and the discovery of the fertility-enhancing property of this remarkable drug, which has brought so much happiness to couples who would otherwise not have had children, was an accident. [12]

Another fertility drug, marketed under the trade name Pergonal, was also created under unusual circumstances. Known as HMG, or human menopausal gonadotropin, this substance was extracted from the urine of post-menopausal women, whose systems carry larger

Cancer Risk from Fertility Drugs

Several studies have shown that there may be a connection between the use of fertility drugs and ovarian cancer. Multiple ovulation and increased levels of FSH and LH are factors that determine this increased risk. Many physicians now recommend limited use of Clomid—for no more than three or four ovulatory cycles. A 1994 study concluded that women who underwent twelve or more cycles of Clomid were more at risk than a woman who had never taken the drug. However, some studies suggest that being infertile is in itself a risk factor for later development of ovarian cancer, particularly if a woman never conceives or carries a baby to term.

amounts of FSH and LH since their ovaries are no longer functioning. In 1949 Italian scientist Piero Donini, of Serono Laboratories in Rome, was the first to prepare the purified HMG. His unlikely but ready source of urine was from a group of nuns in a nearby convent.

Following two years of clinical trials with HMG by Serona, the first baby conceived following ovulation induction with Pergonal was born in 1962. By the mid-1960s, the drug was being prescribed by physicians in Europe and the United States. Urine collection stretched into the tens of millions of gallons to meet the increased demand.

When a woman's ovaries do not respond to clomiphene citrate (trade name Clomid), her physician will likely prescribe Pergonal. Unlike Clomid, which is administered orally in tablet form, Pergonal is one of a group of drugs known as injectable gonadotropins. These drugs are given either intramuscularly—usually deep in the muscle of the buttocks with long needle, or subcutaneously—just under the skin with a much shorter needle. Eventually, the injectable gonadotropins would be produced by genetically engineered cells, making the manufacturers less reliant on obtaining supplies of urine and resulting in a purer form of the drug.

By the late 1960s, both Pergonal and Clomid were the most effective treatments offered by infertility specialists to women who suffered from ovulation disorders. In the decades that followed, thousands of women would undergo hormone therapy, despite the unpleasant side effects, such as hot flashes, headaches, abdominal tenderness and bloating, and mood swings, in hopes of having a baby.

Advancements in Microsurgery

Fertility-enhancing drugs offered hope to women whose reproductive organs were structurally normal, but they could not help women who were infertile due to problems such as blocked or damaged fallopian tubes, scar tissue from surgery or infections, and endometriosis (a condition in which tissue from the uterine lining attaches itself elsewhere in the body, causing inflammation). But diagnosis and treatment of these physical obstacles required that physicians have direct access to a woman's reproductive organs, located in the pelvic cavity.

Since the early 1800s, doctors had been able to examine the pelvic cavity using an endoscope, a device somewhat like a telescope that was inserted through a large incision in the abdominal wall. However, for the patient, such a large incision posed a high risk of death due to blood loss and infection. Furthermore, other abdominal organs, situated above and around the reproductive organs, prevented an unobstructed look at the uterus and ovaries.

The procedure was refined in the 1920s when a British surgeon used gas to expand the abdomen, pushing it away from the internal organs. This allowed for a much improved viewing area for the surgeon. Then in the 1940s, a New York physician devised a method of winding the endoscopic tube through the vagina and the cervix for an interior view of the uterus. The procedure, called culdoscopy, was awkward, though, and with lack of lighting, physicians could not see well enough to make a thorough assessment.

In the late 1950s, Raoul Palmer, a French physician, created the first version of the modern-day laparoscope. By 1964, with the help of Hans Frangenheim, a doctor from West Germany, he had restructured the instrument by adding a miniature light source and replacing the lens and tubing with fiber-optic parts.

While these innovations helped physicians gain better viewing access to the pelvic area, the observation and surgical repair of the minute structures of the reproductive system continued to be a challenge. A fallopian tube, for example, is 4 inches long and less than half an inch in diameter. In earlier times, doctors wore operating glasses, which provided a modest amount of magnification. Microscopes came to use during surgery in

A surgeon uses an instrument known as a laparoscope during surgery. The laparoscope is introduced into the body through a tiny abdominal incision.

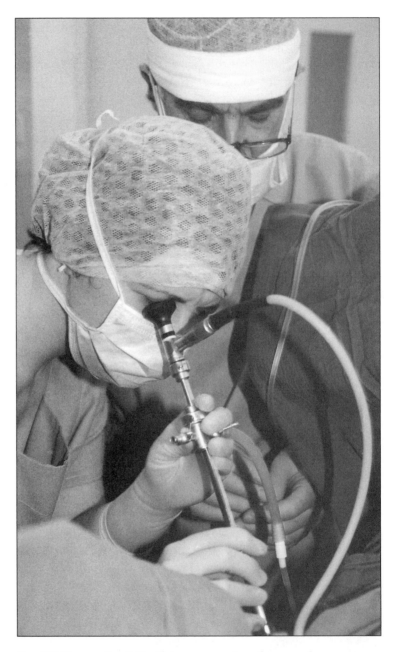

the 1920s, and while this was a step forward, surgeons were still hindered by the lack of microscopic tools, such as surgical needles and thread. By the 1960s, however, manufacturers were able to respond to the call for smaller instruments. They produced needles as thin as a single hair and surgical thread so fine that it was nearly impossible to detect without magnification.

"With the new technology," write the authors of *The Couple's Guide to Fertility*, "came the need for new skills. Surgeons had to learn how to sew using a specially adapted jeweler's forceps or tweezers while looking through the eyepieces of a microscope. After practicing for hundreds of hours in the lab, microsurgeons began performing previously impossible surgical feats, such as repairing ultrathin nerves and blood vessels and removing tiny tumors from the brain." [13]

Correcting Structural Problems with Microsurgery

By the 1970s, microsurgery was being applied to help women who were infertile. In her guide *The Infertility Book: A Comprehensive Medical and Emotional Guide*, Carla Harkness, who has herself experienced infertility, says, "Previously, such surgery [pelvic] was performed without a microscope (macrosurgery) and was not very successful in terms of subsequent pregnancies. The advent of microsurgery provided greater magnification of the affected area, more delicate and precise cutting and suturing, gentler handling of the tissues." [14]

Fallopian Tubes and Fertility

Healthy fallopian tubes are important to a woman's fertility. Funnel-shaped ends (the fimbria) catch the ripened egg when it is released from the ovary. Fluids within the tubes help nurture both egg and sperm. The tubes are lined with tiny, hairlike projections called cilia that aid the movement of sperm toward the egg. If fertilization occurs, the cilia will spur the embryo along its path to the uterus. A woman's fertility can be significantly reduced if the fallopian tubes are damaged; in fact, up to 30 percent of female infertility is due to blocked tubes. Successful treatment by microsurgery depends upon the severity of the damage and where the scar tissue has formed. If the tube has been damaged near the midpoint, that section can be cut out and the healthy ends joined together. More difficult to repair is damage to the fimbria or the lining of the tube itself.

Microsurgery held many other benefits over traditional surgery for the infertility patient. Where once an incision several inches long was necessary, now only a small incision through the navel was needed. Many of these surgeries could also be performed on an outpatient basis—that is, the patient could arrive at the hospital or doctor's office, have the surgery, and return home the same day. In addition, if diagnosis by laparoscopy indicated a need for corrective surgery, the procedure could usually be performed immediately. Most importantly, microsurgery combined with laparoscopy yielded better results in regaining patient fertility, possibly due to reduced formation of scar tissue, which for some patients was the problem in the first place.

The possibilities for treatment opened up even further in 1979 when doctors first used lasers with the laparoscope. The chief advantage of the laser as a cutting instrument was that it could burn away abnormal or unwanted tissue cleanly with minimal bleeding. Surgeons could control the depth of tissue the laser reached, which meant that the surrounding normal tissue—organs and structures like the bowels, fallopian tubes, and blood vessels—were safe from damage. Heat from the laser also sterilized the area, thereby decreasing the chances of infection.

Treating Male Infertility with Surgery and Hormone Therapy

Just as women benefited enormously from advances in surgical and hormonal therapies, so too did men who suffered from infertility. One highly treatable male problem was varicose veins of the scrotum, called *varioceles*. *Varioceles* can cause problems with normal sperm production—chiefly sperm count, but mobility and sperm structure may also be affected. While this effect is not fully understood, the accepted theory is that the pooling of blood in the dilated vessels of the *variocele* raises the temperature of the testicles. Even a small increase in temperature is known to decrease normal sperm production.

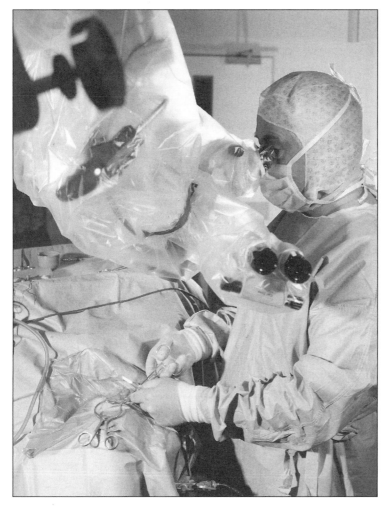

A doctor performing microsurgery uses a large microscope suspended over the patient to magnify the operating area.

Using microsurgical techniques, the doctor will expose the mass of veins and tie them off with sutures. More than 60 percent of men who have the procedure done will see the quality of their sperm improve, and about 40 percent of them will go on to father a child within a year. Microsurgery is also used to clear blockages in the ducts that carry sperm from the testicles to the urethra for ejaculation. It can sometimes remove such blockages, but success rates for this problem are not as high as for the repair of *varioceles*.

Men can also be infertile due to hormonal imbalances, although unlike women, the benefits from the therapy are less clear-cut. The same hormones that induce ovulation in women also play a role in the male's reproductive processes. Specifically, FSH and LH stimulate the production of testosterone in men; testosterone in turn fosters the development of mature, healthy sperm cells. Clomid and Pergonal are the two most common drugs prescribed to increase sperm count. Still, success rates for hormone therapy are not very high when it comes to treating male infertility.

Sometimes, no matter the skill of the surgeon or several cycles of hormone therapy, couples who want a child are disappointed. In some cases, the man and woman have seemingly normal reproductive systems but remain childless. Maranto, in *Quest for Perfection*, explains:

> The formidable complexity of the female reproductive system, involving the brain, various glands and tissues, a battery of hormones, and intricate feedback loops, can confound researchers even today, after eight or nine decades of highly productive probing. Some 30 percent of couples who visit physicians complaining of an inability to conceive are poked, scanned, and tested, only to be told their infertility is idiopathic; that is, its cause cannot be identified. Moreover, the fine points of conception and implantation remain unexplicated.[15]

For such couples, other reproductive technologies, such as in vitro ferilization (IVF), will be their next option.

CHAPTER 3

The Keystone of Assisted Reproduction: In Vitro Fertilization

Although many women achieved pregnancy through artificial insemination, hormone treatments, or surgery, for some couples these treatments were unsuccessful. While in vitro fertilization (IVF) is an invasive and costly procedure, it has become a realistic option for many couples for whom other reproductive technologies have failed. With the development of IVF, problems with damaged fallopian tubes, age-related infertility, or even unexplained infertility could possibly be overcome.

The Early Days of Embryology

Much of the collective knowledge that made IVF possible was gathered through research with animals. The history of IVF began in 1878 with experiments conducted by S.L. Schenk, a Viennese embryologist. Using rabbits and guinea pigs as his subjects, Schenk made several attempts to combine sperm and eggs in a lab

41

dish. The resulting embryos only survived to the two-cell stage, but Schenk's 1880 report noting the feat was widely read and discussed in the scientific community because it was the first successful attempt at fertilizing mammalian eggs in vitro—that is, outside the body.

Soon others were trying to replicate and expand on Schenk's experiments. One of these researchers was M.J. Onanoff. He managed to maintain the embryos created in his laboratory to the eight-cell stage. Why Onanoff's embryos survived so much longer than Schenk's is unclear. Modern-day embryologists assume he must have devised a special solution in which to place the embryos, but no record of that exists. Onanoff also experimented with embryo transfer, a necessary final step in the IVF procedure, by nesting rabbit and guinea pig embryos within the abdominal cavities of his male and female lab animals. These embryos survived longer still.

Ten years later, Heape, the Cambridge biologist who had conducted experiments relating to ovulation, proved that embryo transfers could culminate in live births. Heape removed a batch of fertilized eggs from a female Angora rabbit by flushing them out with a saline solution and then placed them into another rabbit. To make certain that any young that came from the transferred embryos were those of the donor rabbit, he used a different variety of rabbit as host. Four weeks later, the host mother, a Belgian hare, gave birth to six young. Heape notified the Royal Society of London for the Improvement of Natural Knowledge of his successful experiment. The Royal Society published his letter, in which he wrote, "In this preliminary note I wish merely to record an experiment by which it is shown that it is possible to make use of the uterus of one variety of rabbit as a medium for the growth and complete fetal development of fertilized ova of another variety of rabbit." [16]

Laying the Groundwork for IVF Procedures

For the next forty years, many researchers would try to imitate Heape. Not until American biologist Gregory

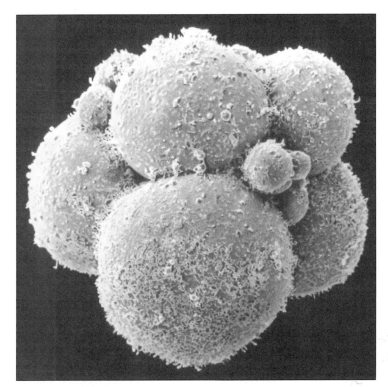

A three-day-old embryo created through in vitro fertilization. The procedure involves introducing into the uterus an embryo created outside the body.

Pincus developed his own studies would anyone match Heape's skillful manipulation of mammalian eggs. Pincus held degrees in genetics and animal physiology and had studied with noted biologist F.H.A. Marshall at Cambridge University. Pincus was interested in every aspect of eggs. One colleague referred to Pincus's lab as a "place where the mammalian egg was studied and honored."[17] In addition, Pincus was interested in embryo transfer and tried to replicate Heape's results.

After several failures, Pincus finally devised an approach that got positive results. Working alongside a colleague, E.V. Enzmann, Pincus developed a procedure whereby several unfertilized eggs from a rabbit were retrieved, placed in a shallow dish, and then a solution containing sperm was added. After waiting for about twenty minutes and observing fertilization take place, Pincus inserted the fertilized eggs into the fallopian tube of another rabbit. As Heape had done, to make certain that any babies were those of the donor rabbit rather than the host female, Pincus and Enzmann used different varieties for host and donor. These experiments worked: That is, the host rabbit delivered babies that carried the physical traits of the donor variety of rabbit.

After Pincus's success, it was only a matter of time before IVF was attempted with human eggs. Pincus himself carried out several preliminary trials, but it was John Rock and Miriam Menkin of Harvard Medical School who, in the late 1940s, earned the distinction of creating the first human embryos in vitro. Using eggs that had been donated by patients at the Boston Free Hospital for Women, they experimented with the solution the eggs were placed in, how long sperm and egg

Dr. John Rock (shown) and Dr. Miriam Menkin created the first human embryos in vitro in the 1940s.

had contact with one another, and with various concentrations of sperm. Of the 138 eggs on which they experimented, however, only three were fertilized, and these embryos did not develop past a handful of cells.

Maranto comments on the outgrowth of these first tentative steps: "In vitro fertilization in humans, however, was by no means a done deal."

> Eggs and sperm turned out to be notoriously temperamental, performing differently in the hands of every researcher. Over the next decade, scientists engaged in repeats, reruns, redos. They muddled, goofed, and bollixed things up more often than they attained the outcome they wanted. Perplexed by every failure, urged onward by every success, researchers around the world raced to reach the goal—a combined in vitro fertilization and embryo transfer resulting in a live birth—before anyone else.[18]

From Mice Embryos to Humans

In 1951 Robert Edwards, a graduate student at the Institute of Animal Genetics at Edinburgh University, was aiming toward that goal of a successful human IVF birth. Early on in his research, Edwards hoped he could apply the results from mice to the problem of human infertility. For example, one of the key factors would be the ability to manipulate events necessary for fertilization, beginning with ovulation.

One thing Edwards had learned about mice was that the females tended to ovulate at night, which meant retrieving eggs at midnight or later. Desiring to keep a more normal schedule, he injected the mice with gonadotropic hormones to see if he could sway the pattern of ovulation. In doing so, he also hoped to achieve superovulation, the production of large numbers of eggs, thereby gaining control of not only the timing of ovulation but increasing the number of eggs available to work with as well.

Through his work with mice embryos, Edwards was essentially developing a protocol for human IVF. He was convinced that the technique of fertilizing eggs in culture dishes and then transferring the embryos back into the female mice could be accomplished with humans. It is interesting to note that Edwards did not have a medical doctor's degree. "So the push for human IVF did not come from within the medical establishment," explains Lee M. Silver. "It came instead from a basic researcher who understood and appreciated the striking similarity in biology that exists between humans and all other mammals."[19]

Harvesting Human Eggs

Edwards single-mindedly forged ahead, knowing he would need an endless supply of human eggs. He arranged for several gynecological surgeons to provide him with ovarian tissue taken from their patients who had, for medical reasons, undergone oophorectomies (removal of the ovaries). This arrangement presented two problems, which he attacked right away: bringing an unripe, harvested egg to maturity before fertilization in a petri dish and finding the right culture medium in which to nourish the egg.

What Edwards had hoped was that more eggs would be available for the in vitro process if they could be matured in a laboratory setting instead of using the single ripe egg most women produced each month. Even though Edwards managed to ripen human eggs in his laboratory, however, this proved of little help in the end. Several animal researchers had demonstrated that eggs brought to maturity in a test tube and then fertilized would develop for only a brief time before dying, and Edwards found that this held true with human eggs as well. Edwards decided that if the process were to succeed, he must use an egg that had matured in the ovary, not in the laboratory.

The question then became how to tell when an egg was ripe for fertilization if it was still inside a woman's body. The solution to the dilemma of how to monitor the status of an egg came in 1968 when Edwards met

Related IVF Techniques

The standard IVF procedure has generated a variety of related techniques, each with its own representative acronym and each appropriate in addressing different fertility problems.

GIFT (Gamete intrafallopian transfer)

The procedure begins like an IVF cycle with the use of fertility drugs to induce superovulation and the retrieval of eggs and sperm. But instead of fertilizing the eggs in the laboratory, the sperm and eggs are simply mixed together and then placed directly into the fallopian tube via laparoscopy. The chief advantage of this procedure is that it does not require the technical expertise in the laboratory of standard IVF. Also, some experts believe that the embryo will be more likely to develop if it is exposed to the natural fluids of the fallopian tubes.

ZIFT (Zygote intrafallopian transfer)

This procedure is exactly the same as GIFT except that the sperm and egg are joined in fertilization but have not yet begun to divide. The resulting zygote is then transferred into the fallopian tube. Like GIFT, it is hoped that the natural environment of the fallopian tubes will aid in embryo development. But unlike GIFT, ZIFT allows physicians to determine that fertilization has occurred before the embryo is transferred.

ICSI (Introcytoplasmic sperm injection)

A single sperm is injected directly into the center of the egg, therefore bypassing the need for the sperm to penetrate the egg on its own. This procedure can be of benefit to couples who experience male-factor infertility, such as fewer or slower-swimming sperm.

PZD (Partial zona dissection)

An opening is made in the outer gelatinous coating of the egg (the zona), either with chemicals or a microneedle, making it easier for the sperm to access the cell membrane. It has been an effective procedure but its use is declining as success rates for ICSI have improved and are generally more consistent.

SUZI (Subzonal insertion)

This technique differs from PZD in that sperm are actually injected through the zona and placed close to the cell membrane. Like PZD, it has often been used in couples with severe male-factor infertility or failed attempts at IVF. However, since success rates depend on the number of sperm injected, a chief disadvantage is that almost half of the fertilized embryos must be discarded because they have been fertilized by more than one sperm. This condition, known as polyspermy, results in an abnormal embryo.

Following fertilization with ICSI, PZD, or SUZI, the embryo is transferred just as it would be in a standard IVF procedure.

Patrick Steptoe, an English gynecologist who was adept at using the laparoscope. Edwards posed a question to Steptoe: Would it be possible to monitor ovarian activity with a laparoscope? Steptoe considered and then agreed it might be, under the right conditions.

Robert Edwards and IVF

In the book A Matter of Life: The Story of a Medical Breakthrough *coauthored with his partner Patrick Steptoe and published in 1980, Robert Edwards reflects on the development of IVF and the opportunities it has offered to humankind.*

The cure of certain kinds of infertility is not the only advance we now have within our grasp. There are so many other opportunities. We have the chance to look at the causes of some other human disorders—those upsets where the smallest change in the number of chromosomes of the fetus can disastrously affect its well-being. . . . I still believe that the secrets of the causes of these disorders lie in those ripening eggs, in those chromosomes moving so steadily through the egg as it undergoes its ripening process. We can turn to a closer examination of these problems.

These are wonderful opportunities which, if successful, can alleviate, indeed prevent, much human suffering. Even so, there are other major advantages to be made, other challenges elsewhere. I often think of that embryo which grew for nine days in our culture, of how it wriggled out of its membrane and expanded beautifully. Consider again that embryo: within it all the stem cells of the body's organs were differentiating and growing, appearing steadily, one by one. This, for me, was excitement magnified because it offered all the beginnings of human embryology to us; here was the chance of watching and analyzing the appearances and growth of the different tissues of the body—the heart, the blood system, the brain. These tissues could one day form in front of our very eyes!

Patrick Steptoe (left) and Robert Edwards announce the success of their IVF experiments in 1969.

Together they devised a plan for Steptoe, using his laparoscope, to harvest ripe eggs from human ovaries. Edwards decided to use hormones to control the menstrual cycle and to artificially prompt ovulation. This way, they would know when to perform the procedure. After perfectly timing the egg retrieval, their success depended on Steptoe's skill with the laparoscope. He would need to remove the eggs right from the ovary without harming them. They created a bevel-tipped, hollow tube no larger around than a small knitting needle. They fitted it to the end of the laparoscope, which Steptoe would manipulate, then gently suck up the egg from its follicle.

Edwards also needed to find a culture medium that would support the egg until it was fertilized and then afterward as an embryo. Since he first began working with human eggs, Edwards had been searching for just the right formula that would nurture the embryo until it was at the stage—either eight or sixteen cells—when it would normally attach itself to the wall of the uterus. If that milestone could be reached, it was not too far-fetched to believe that an embryo transfer could be successful.

For the culture medium, Edwards settled on a basic mixture with ingredients similar to the fluids found in the fallopian tubes. He based his choice on the work of M.C. Chang, a scientist who had shown that these fluids help the sperm shed its outer coating, a step that facilitates penetration of the egg making fertilization possible.

The plan worked. By the early 1970s, Edwards and Steptoe were regularly creating embryos whose cells doubled several times over. Soon they were transferring the eight- and sixteen-celled embryos back into the prospective mothers. However, all of the pregnancies ended in spontaneous abortion shortly after implantation. Edwards scanned the data to determine what had gone wrong. He finally concluded that the hormonal drug therapy, which was administered to promote superovulation, was harming the endometrium, or lining of the uterus. Just as the embryo was ready to implant, the uterus was shedding the lining that the embryo needed for nourishment. In other words, the patient was beginning her menstrual period almost immediately after receiving the embryo.

Over the next few years Edwards and Steptoe tried a variety of hormone therapies to bypass the problem, and finally, in 1975, they achieved their first IVF pregnancy. But misfortune struck when they discovered that the thirteen-week-old embryo had attached itself in the woman's fallopian tube rather than her uterus. This phenomenon, called an ectopic pregnancy, endangered the health and life of the mother. The pregnancy had to be aborted.

The First Test-Tube Baby

In spite of this setback, Steptoe and Edwards pressed on. Because of the previous problems, they abandoned the routine of fertility drugs and decided to rely on a woman's natural cycle. While this meant there would be only one egg to retrieve, and therefore only one opportunity each cycle, the pair was confident. They would measure the patient's LH level to predict when ovulation would take place and, with Steptoe's expertise, snatch the single egg at the right moment.

By the fall of 1977, their new protocol was in place. They selected twenty-two-year-old Lesley Brown for the procedure. Brown, infertile because of blockages in her fallopian tubes, was a perfect candidate for IVF since her reproductive organs were otherwise normal. In November that year, after monitoring her hormone levels for the LH surge that indicates ovulation is imminent, Steptoe retrieved one ripe egg from Brown's ovary. Edwards placed it in a petri dish along with sperm contributed by Brown's husband, John.

Through the lens of a microscope, Edwards observed the egg as it was fertilized and began to double, and then double again. A few days later, Steptoe inserted a catheter

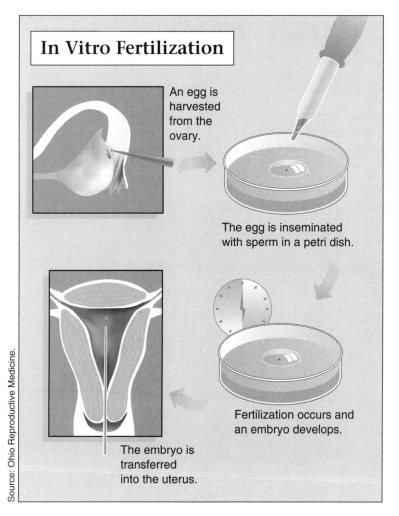

In Vitro Fertilization

An egg is harvested from the ovary.

The egg is inseminated with sperm in a petri dish.

Fertilization occurs and an embryo develops.

The embryo is transferred into the uterus.

Source: Ohio Reproductive Medicine.

containing the embryo into Brown's cervical opening, and with a plunger at the end of the catheter, he released the embryo into the uterus. Then the waiting began.

Through the rest of November and into December, Edwards eyed Brown's blood and urine test results for a slow rise in progesterone levels that would indicate pregnancy. When the levels rose as expected, Edwards and Steptoe knew that their patient was pregnant, but given the many failed attempts at IVF, they tried to keep the pregnancy a secret, at least for the first few months, until further tests indicated the fetus was developing normally. Word soon leaked out, however. The Browns

IVF: The Foundation of Reproductive Technology

Virtually every assisted reproductive technology (ART) available today exists due to the research following the 1978 birth of Louise Brown, the first so-called test-tube baby. And that achievement itself was preceded by many years of scientific investigations dating back to the 1600s. Susan Lewis Cooper and Ellen Sarasohn Glazer explain in their book *Choosing Assisted Reproduction* that "*in vitro* fertilization forms the cornerstone of the new reproductive technologies. When Louise Brown [was born] . . . few people, if any, appreciated the range of reproductive possibilities that would result from this new technology. Once eggs could be removed from a woman's body and fertilized outside it, the genetic and gestational components of motherhood could be separated. This separation produced an array of reproductive options."

Louise Brown, the first test-tube baby, was born on July 25, 1978.

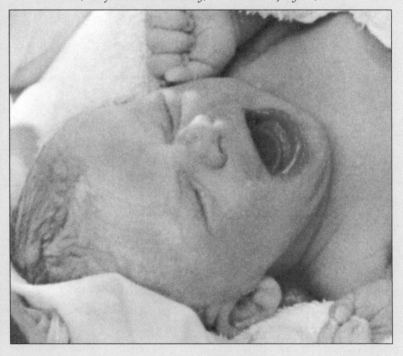

were hounded by the press at the hospital and at their home.

A few days before Brown's due date, Steptoe scheduled a cesarean section. He wanted to take no chances with any complications from a natural delivery. When baby Louise Brown arrived on July 25, 1978, for Edwards and Steptoe it was the finale of a ten-year collaboration and nearly a century of research by their many predecessors. Silver describes the event in this way:

> This birth represented the culmination of more than a decade of work on human eggs and embryos by Steptoe and Edwards, who should be recognized as the founders of the new age of reprogenetics. The significance of their feat cannot be overemphasized. IVF—the term now used to describe the entire process from egg and sperm collection to embryo placement in the uterus—was developed originally for the purpose of curing one type of infertility. But what IVF does inherently, as well, is provide access to the egg and embryo. [20]

This access to the egg was only the beginning. Once doctors could remove eggs from a woman's body and manipulate them in the laboratory, a wide array of options became available to infertile couples. Refinements of the basic IVF procedures would make parenthood possible even for people with extreme cases of infertility.

CHAPTER 4

Surrogacy, Egg Donation, and Embryo Adoption

While IVF has been the answer for many couples' infertility, it has not been able to help everyone who desires a child. Third-party methods—surrogacy, egg donation, and embryo adoption—are proving to be viable alternatives for couples who are unable to have a child by other methods. These new technologies are similar in concept to one of the oldest forms of reproductive technology, donor insemination.

Depending on IVF

All three of these options (excluding traditional surrogacy) depend on the basic techniques of IVF, which involves the fertilization of an egg outside a woman's body. Geoffrey Sher, Virginia Marriage Davis, and Jean Stoess, coauthors of *In Vitro Fertilization: The A.R.T. of Making Babies*, explain the impact of IVF on expanding the range of infertility solutions:

> Only a few years ago, women who did not have a healthy uterus and those who could not produce healthy eggs had the lowest chance of having their own baby. Now quite paradoxically, through the advent of egg donation and

IVF/surrogacy (IVF third-party parenting), these women have the greatest chance by far of conceiving, far greater than with any other cause of infertility.[21]

Traditional Surrogacy

In its traditional form, surrogacy is relatively uncomplicated and was likely used even in ancient times. A surrogate mother agrees to have a child for another woman who, for various reasons, is either unable to get pregnant or carry a child to term. The traditional surrogate mother is a donor in the sense that she is offering both her egg and the use of her uterus.

Through most of human history, most cases of surrogacy remained unrecorded and under a cloak of secrecy. These surrogacy arrangements were made between

Infertile couples have the option of selecting a surrogate mother to carry and give birth to their child.

people who had close ties to each other, and it more than likely did not include the exchange of money. It is probable that an infertile woman asked a sister or close friend to bear a child on her behalf. The child carried by the surrogate mother might even have been fathered by the surrogate's husband, in which case the baby was not biologically related to the infertile couple at all.

In other cases, the partner of the infertile woman may have agreed to father a child with the surrogate mother. This particular choice became more acceptable with the availability of artificial insemination. It eliminated the need for sexual contact between surrogate mother and biological father yet allowed the baby to be genetically related to one half of the infertile couple.

Surrogacy Contracts

Surrogate motherhood has continued to be an option for infertile couples. However, because of questions about the legal status of the surrogate mother, it became necessary to legalize the arrangement with a contract in an attempt to protect the rights of the people involved. In recent times, especially when surrogate mothers are often not part of the family or even known beforehand to the prospective parents, some sort of legal planning became necessary. Noel Keane, a Michigan attorney, in 1976 negotiated and drafted the first formal contract between a surrogate mother and a married couple in the United States.

In the early days of contractual surrogacy, however, many people were unaware it existed; the idea of surrogacy had yet to be assimilated into everyday language. In fact, the phrase *surrogate mother* only first appeared in print in a June 19, 1978, *Time* magazine article entitled "The Cloning Era Is Almost Here." It took seven years and a high-profile legal battle to bring surrogacy to the forefront of public awareness.

The Fight for Baby M

In 1985 a New Jersey couple—Bill Stern, a research biochemist, and his wife Elizabeth, a pediatrician—

Predicting Surrogacy as an Outgrowth of IVF Technology

In an article titled "Moving Toward the Clonal Man" published in Atlantic Monthly *in May 1971, James D. Watson, English scientist and codiscoverer of the DNA double helix, anticipates that IVF technology would eventually lead to a practical use of surrogate mothers.*

Clearly, if Edwards and Steptoe succeed [at creating a test-tube baby], their success will be followed up in many other places. The number of such infertile women, while small on a relative percentage basis, is likely to be large on an absolute basis. Within the United States there could be 100,000 or so women who would like a similar chance to have their own babies. At the same time, we must anticipate strong, if not hysterical, reactions from many quarters. The certainty that the ready availability of this medical technique will open up the possibility of hiring out unrelated women to carry a baby to term is bound to outrage many people. For there is absolutely no reason why the blastocyst need be implanted in the same woman from whom the pre-ovulatory eggs were obtained. Many women with anatomical complications which prohibit successful childbearing might be strongly tempted to find a suitable surrogate. And it is easy to imagine that other women who just don't want the discomforts of pregnancy would also seek this very different form of motherhood.

contracted with Mary Beth Whitehead to act as a surrogate mother. Whitehead agreed to be artificially inseminated with Stern's sperm and, following the birth of the baby, surrender it to the Sterns. The couple agreed to pay all expenses related to the pregnancy and delivery, and once the baby was in the Sterns' custody, Whitehead would be paid a fee of ten thousand dollars.

Whitehead gave birth to a daughter on March 27, 1986. Unexpectedly, however, she named the baby Sara Elizabeth, refused payment, and refused to give up the child. A long battle for custody began, and after a six-week trial, the judge ruled in favor of the Sterns. Calling the surrogacy contract valid and enforceable, he terminated Whitehead's parental claim and granted Bill Stern permanent custody of the child he and Elizabeth had named Melissa. Following the verdict, Elizabeth Stern signed papers naming her the adoptive mother of the baby.

This highly publicized dispute set off a chain of arguments regarding the validity of surrogate contracts and questions about whether surrogacy was an immoral practice that, among other things, exploited women. Opponents believed that it reduced women to the status of mere baby breeders. Others claimed it took financial advantage of poor women who, they said, were more likely to act as surrogate mothers. Supporters, however, asserted that it was a logical and necessary option and could work if regulated properly. Moreover, for many infertile couples, traditional surrogacy renowned their only chance to have a baby.

Elizabeth and Bill Stern won a custody battle in 1986 after the surrogate mother they had contracted to carry their child refused to surrender the infant.

Gestational Surrogacy

IVF technology, meanwhile, was becoming more refined, and as this developed a new form of surrogacy, known

as gestational surrogacy, was created. In this type of surrogacy, the surrogate mother provides the use of her uterus only, rather than also contributing an egg. Women who stood to benefit from this type of surrogacy were those who still had functioning ovaries but, due to a medical condition, previous surgery, or some uterine defect, could not bear a child. The advantage gestational surrogacy held over traditional surrogacy was that it offered couples the option of having a child that was genetically related to both husband and wife, not just the husband. Gestational surrogacy involves egg retrieval from the woman seeking to have a child and fertilization in the laboratory with her husband's sperm. The resulting embryo or embryos are then implanted into the surrogate mother's uterus rather than the woman from whom the egg was retrieved, as happens in a normal IVF cycle.

Defining Motherhood

While this new technology was the answer for many infertile couples, it raised questions about the very meaning of motherhood. It had seemed that a gestational surrogacy arrangement could alleviate disputes over who the "real" mother was, because the resulting baby was not genetically related to the surrogate. But in a 1993 case, a gestational surrogate mother attempted to claim parental rights for the baby boy she carried, even though she had no biological connection to him. According to California law, Anna Johnson, the surrogate mother, and Crispina Calvert, the genetic mother, each met one of the criteria used to establish motherhood. The California Supreme Court had to choose which factor carried more weight—the contribution of genes or the act of giving birth. The court ruled in favor of Calvert, explaining that the intent of the contracting couple must be considered. It held that the woman who hired a surrogate and planned to "bring about the birth of a child she intended to raise as her own is the natural mother under California law."[22] In effect, a gestational carrier had no right to maternal claims after the baby was born.

It has been difficult for physicians to establish guidelines that can match the rapid pace of IVF-related technology and help patients evade potential legal wrangles. One physician, William Andereck, at a 1993 medical conference, presented his advice concerning gestational surrogacy:

> The two-out-of-three rule basically looks at these three elements: the egg, the sperm, and the gestational component [the uterus]. If at all possible, I recommend that at least two of these three components be contributed by the intended parents. If they can only contribute one, by all means please try not to get the other two contributed by the same person. [23]

As the expanding IVF technology raised concerns about the meaning of motherhood, it also allowed for some unprecedented events. In 1991, for example, Arlette Schweitzer of Rapid City, South Dakota, became the gestational carrier for her own grandchildren. Her daughter, Christa Uchytil, had been born without a uterus. The twin babies were conceived in vitro using Uchytil's eggs and her husband's sperm. The embryos were then transferred to Schweitzer's uterus. Schweitzer and her daughter did not have a written contract because as Schweitzer said, "It didn't have to be [written]. We know each other so well and that is one of the benefits of not hiring a surrogate." [24]

Egg Donation as an Alternative to Surrogacy

Gestational surrogacy is an option when a woman has functioning ovaries. However, many otherwise healthy women are infertile because they are either unable to produce their own eggs or the eggs they produce cannot be used. These women have the physical capability of bearing a child, but suffer from premature ovarian failure or early menopause, have experienced previous IVF failures, or are carriers of a genetic disorder that they do not want to risk passing on to their offspring.

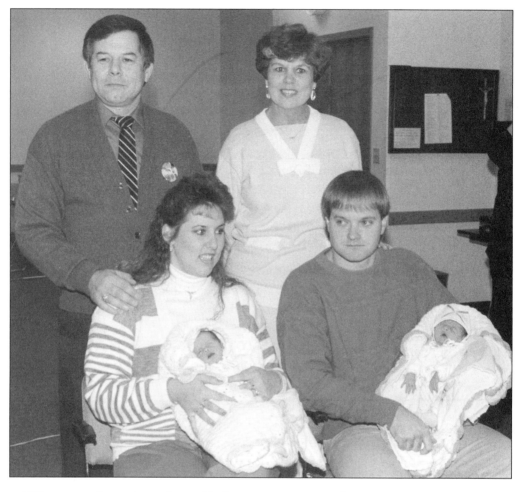

When egg donation, also called ovum or oocyte donation, became available in 1984, it offered a viable option
for such women. This option offered several advantages
over both types of surrogacy. First, since the egg donor
usually remains anonymous, her role is over once the
eggs are removed from her body. Thus, parents do not
have to deal with the social complications that can
attend even a passing connection to a third party.
Second, the infertile woman who will carry the embryo
resulting from the donated egg becomes, in one way
the baby's biological mother. Finally, there are many
more women willing to donate eggs than to be surrogate mothers.

*Arlette Schweitzer
(right, standing) was
the first woman to give
birth to her own
grandchildren.
Schweitzer acted as a
surrogate mother for
her infertile daughter.*

Egg-Donation Protocol

The major challenge in developing the technology that made egg donation (and gestational surrogacy) possible was to synchronize the cycles of two women at once—the donor and recipient. The procedure is more complex in comparison to traditional surrogacy, in which only one woman's cycle must be considered.

Overcoming the challenge of perfect timing required persistent trial and error. It also required a solid background in IVF technology. Two Australian scientists—Alan Trounson, an embryologist, and his colleague Carl Wood, a physician—had been one of the medical teams in the world working to produce the first IVF baby. When the announcement came in 1978 of the birth of Louise Brown, they had not been far behind Edwards and Steptoe. In fact, in 1980 they achieved the first IVF birth in Australia, and only the third in the world.

Wood and Trounson then turned their attention to women who were infertile because of ill-functioning ovaries, premature menopause, or had no ovaries at all. IVF had been proven to work for women who produced eggs, but women whose reproductive problems were so fundamental needed another answer. After five years and numerous attempts to establish the right mix of hormones and timing, the result was the 1983 birth of the world's first donor-egg baby. Woods and Trounson had established a protocol for egg donation that would become standard procedure everywhere.

Much of that procedure was similar in concept to basic IVF. Hormones are administered to the egg donor to ripen her egg follicles. When she is near ovulation, several eggs are removed with a hollow needle attached to a laparoscope. The eggs are then mixed with the sperm of the recipient's husband and fertilized. Meanwhile the recipient has received hormonal injections to prepare the endometrium for implantation and nurturing of the embryos. Once the embryos have been transferred, the hormone regimen is continued to sustain a favorable uterine environment so the embryo will be nurtured and continue to grow.

Cryopreservation of Embryos and Eggs

While Woods and Trounson were developing their egg-donation protocol, they also attempted to establish a routine of freezing the extra embryos. Since the hormones administered to the egg donor normally caused the release of several eggs per cycle (known as superovulation), the resulting fertilized embryos would be wasted unless they were all implanted. But implanting too many embryos at one time put the health of the mother and the babies at risk. The human body did not evolve to nurture more than two or three fetuses at once. Furthermore, multiple fetuses may experience retarded lung development, bleeding in the brain, and premature birth. If the babies do survive after birth, they may suffer from long-term problems such as cerebral palsy,

Inconsistent State Surrogacy Laws

While the Baby M case was a rare example of surrogacy gone sour, the notoriety surrounding the case provoked many states into enacting laws regarding surrogacy. In 1988 Michigan became the first state to make arranging a surrogacy contract for money a felony. An attorney or other person managing such an arrangement faces a fifty-thousand-dollar fine and five years in prison. The couple and surrogate could face a ten-thousand-dollar fine and a year in prison.

By 2003 twenty-three states had adopted surrogacy laws, but these vary widely from state to state. For instance, Arizona and the District of Columbia banned surrogacy contracts outright. These two states, along with Indiana, Kentucky, Louisiana, Michigan, Nebraska, New York, North Dakota, Utah, Virginia, and Washington, ruled that paid and/or unpaid surrogacy contracts are void and therefore unenforceable. This means that the surrogate mother could change her mind after the baby is born without penalty.

When the New Jersey Supreme Court made its decision regarding Baby M, it interpreted the surrogacy contract as the sale of a child. It refused to uphold the contract, since baby selling is illegal in all fifty states. Surrogacy laws in eight states now ban payment to the surrogate for anything other than related expenses, and ten states ban payment to an agent who matches couples with surrogates.

blindness, and learning disabilities. There was a practical side to freezing the extra embryos: It could save women from undergoing another cycle of hormones and another laparoscopy if the first embryo implantation failed.

Woods and Trounson knew that as of 1971, mouse embryos had been successfully cryopreserved and that subsequently embryos of larger animals, such as rabbits, sheep, goats, and cows, had also been successfully preserved. They believed the same could be done for human embryos. Once again, they relied on trial and error to discover a procedure that worked. Attention to details was critical, such as the chemical composition of the liquid for storing the embryos and controlling the rate of temperature change during freezing and thawing.

In the beginning, the odds were against many embryos surviving the thawing process. For example, when Trounson and Woods thawed 40 two-to-eight-celled embryos from a batch of 230, only 23 remained undamaged. In spite of these odds, one of Trounson's early frozen embryos was implanted successfully, and on March 28, 1984, Zoe Leyland was the first human born to develop from a frozen embryo.

Over the next few years, as the technology for freezing embryos improved, scientists anticipated another use for it—freezing eggs. One advantage they saw was that it gave women a kind of fertility insurance. A woman who wished to delay childbearing for some reason could do so without fear that the natural falloff in egg production that accompanies aging would deprive her of children altogether. It would also be a boon to women who were facing possible infertility from cancer or other medical problems.

However, eggs proved to be extremely difficult to freeze without fatally damaging them. The problem seems to lie with the physical composition of eggs, making them ultrasensitive to freezing and thawing, more so than the hardier sperm or even the delicate embryo. Some researchers speculate that the egg is more vulner-

Artificial Wombs: In the Future for Humans?

In 1997 Japanese scientists developed an artificial womb that sustained goat fetuses (which had already spent most of their gestation inside their mothers) for three weeks. When the goats were removed, some lived only a few days but others lived for a little longer. The artificial uterus is a rectangular-shaped plastic box filled with body-temperature amniotic fluid. The fetus's umbilical cord is connected to a dialysis machine that cleans its blood and replaces oxygen. Scientists involved in the project had experimented for more than ten years and estimated that it would be at least another ten years before it would have practical use for human fetuses.

able because it is a single cell, it is filled with liquid, and its chromosomes are exposed. At any rate, eggs are likely to be destroyed in the freezing process, and success rates with frozen eggs are not very promising. Only about forty births worldwide have been reported from frozen eggs. Still, researchers like Thomas Kim of a Los Angeles fertility clinic, and Eleonora Porcu at the University of Bologna in Italy claim, that recent technical developments should improve the success rate. The protocols Kim and Porcu employ differ mostly in the speed with which eggs are frozen. Kim's approach is to freeze the eggs quickly in about a ten-minute span, while Porcu advocates a slower, two-hour approach. Kim minimizes the significance of this difference, saying "The bottom line is, Can you produce a baby? We say yes." [25]

Embryo Adoption

Although doctors have been comparatively successful in using frozen embryos, this technology presents an unanticipated problem: A large number of frozen embryos are being accumulated in storage banks around the world. Many couples who have had children through IVF or who have stopped treatment will have leftover embryos. One solution to this problem is to donate the extra embryos to other infertile couples.

Known as embryo adoption, this method can help a couple when the woman is unable to produce her own eggs and her partner is unable to produce sperm.

The first embryo adoption birth occurred in 1984. Still, while embryo adoption presents an obvious solution to the problem of leftover embryos, the procedure has not become the popular option it was once expected to become. As of 1997, only 150 babies had been born from donated embryos. In an audit completed by the Monash University IVF clinic in Australia, the statistics match what seems to be the overall trend: Couples are choosing to dispose of their frozen embryos rather than donate them. From January 1991 to July 2002, out of 1,246 couples, 1,116 opted to discard their embryos while the remaining 130 couples donated a total of 425 embryos.

A couple gives a thermos containing frozen embryos to a lab technician. Couples have the option of putting leftover frozen embryos up for adoption.

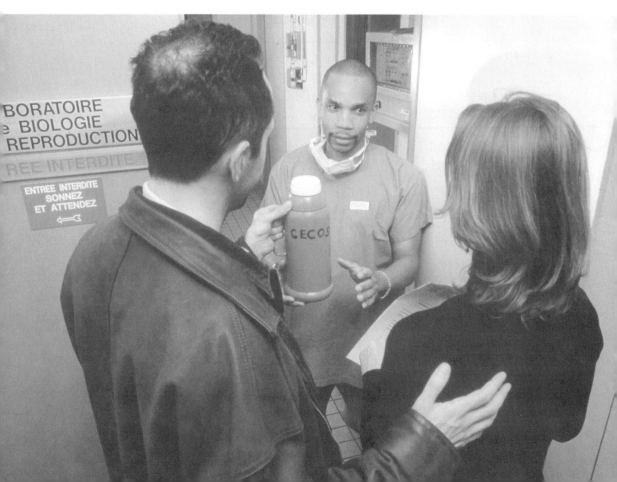

Cooper and Glazer offer a possible explanation of why more couples are not offering their frozen embryos for adoption:

> One explanation is that because most couples with frozen embryos that have been stored over two years have children, they have living examples of what an embryo can become and they can no longer imagine giving up a child like the one they see in front of them . . . [and] . . . couples who have no children but have embryos in storage may not be able to live with the possibility that another couple could raise their genetic child while they themselves remain childless. [26]

The Future of IVF Technology

IVF technology opened the door to a wide range of reproductive options for infertile couples. For many, it created an opportunity to have a child they might never have had otherwise. The ability to move the act of fertilization from within the human body and manipulate it in a laboratory setting allowed physicians to bypass many major physical barriers to conception. Couples for whom there was previously no hope—where the female partner could not produce healthy eggs, for example—have been helped by this technology.

Furthermore, one of the most recent and ongoing developments in IVF technology, known as preimplantation genetic diagnosis, promises to assist couples who wish to have healthy children and avoid passing on any genetic diseases they may carry. It has become a reality because IVF enables scientists to work directly with a living human embryo, something that has never been possible before now.

CHAPTER 5

Preventing Inherited Disease: Preimplantation Genetic Diagnosis

As IVF and other reproductive technologies have become more commonplace, researchers are turning their attention to ways in which they may help couples who are not technically infertile but who have made a conscious decision not to have children for reasons of genetics. Such couples include those with a family history of genetic disorders, and older mothers who are more likely to conceive a child with genetic defects. Some are afraid of the possibility of passing the defective gene to their offspring. Others may already have an affected child and do not want to bear another one with the same abnormality. According to HELP—Health Education Library for People:

> These couples are often faced with attempting a type of
> "Russian roulette" to have children, many times having
> to confront the difficult decision to terminate an affected

pregnancy. Consider a woman known to be carrying the gene for hemophilia. She has a 50% risk of an affected male in each pregnancy. While her daughters have a 50% risk of being carriers, they are going to be clinically normal. She may not wish to become pregnant if she has to make decisions about an affected child in a viable pregnancy. [27]

Limited Options

Previously there were only two options for determining genetic defects in a fetus. The first was a biopsy of the placenta, called chorionic villus sampling, in which a fragment of tissue was removed from the placenta and fetal cells present in the sample were examined under a microscope for genetic abnormalities. The other was amniocentesis, which involved using a long needle to withdraw a small amount of amniotic fluid surrounding the fetus. Fetal cells found in the fluid were then tested for their genetic content.

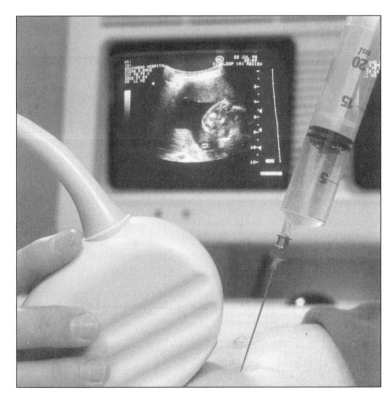

A doctor uses a syringe to withdraw for analysis some of the amniotic fluid surrounding a woman's fetus.

Both tests increased the risk of miscarriage. But the bigger problem was that for relatively accurate results, the tests had to be performed when the pregnancy was already well underway, usually around the third month. This meant that if a problem was discovered, couples were faced with an agonizing choice. They could continue the pregnancy, knowing the child would have some sort of deformity, or they could choose to abort the baby, which for some was an unacceptable option.

The newest IVF-related procedure, called preimplantation genetic diagnosis (PGD), can save couples from having to make such decisions. PGD differs from these older tests because it allows an embryo to be tested in the early-cell stage of development. If it carries a genetic disease, the embryo does not have to be transferred into the uterus for implantation, thus preventing a pregnancy before it begins.

The Development of PGD

Gina Maranto describes the development of PGD as the point "where molecular biology, genetic medicine, and IVF converge."[28] James Trefil, professor of physics at George Mason University in Fairfax, Virginia, and author of numerous scientific books, also comments on the origins of PGD:

> Back in the 1970s, science made advances in two areas that seemed, on the surface, unrelated—but which have veered ever closer to each other. One was a growing understanding of, and ability to manipulate, deoxyribonucleic acid (DNA), the molecule that provides our genetic code. The other involved the advent of in vitro fertilization (IVF), the technology responsible for Louise Brown and nearly a million babies since.[29]

In 1989 Alan Handyside and his team working in a London hospital were the first to use PGD successfully, and it was based on determining the gender of embryos. Handyside's patients who volunteered for the first clinical test were carriers of a genetic disease that would manifest itself in boys but not girls. All doctors

Alan Handyside and his team were the first to successfully use an IVF procedure known as preimplantation genetic diagnosis.

had to do was determine the presence or absence of a Y chromosome—the indicator of a male embryo—on the IVF embryos and then implant the female embryos. The mothers were assured of delivering disease-free children because the babies were girls.

This first use of PGD to avoid implanting male embryos helped couples avoid having children who would suffer from devastating disabilities. These types of diseases include fragile X syndrome, Duchenne muscular dystrophy, hemophilia A, and retinitis pigmentosa. By 1994 approximately thirty children worldwide had been born following genetic screening with PGD. By the middle of 2001, the number had climbed to five hundred.

Analyzing a Single Cell

PGD involves chromosomal and genetic analysis of a single cell from an early embryo prior to implantation

Using PGD for Trait Selection

Susan Lewis Cooper and Ellen Sarasohn Glazer, authors of Choosing Assisted Reproduction: Social, Emotional, and Ethical Considerations, *describe a future in which PGD may used by couples to selectively choose the traits they would like their offspring to have.*

Although scientists have not yet mapped the entire human genome, it will probably not be too long before they can do so. Soon they will be able to determine physical, intellectual, and perhaps emotional and social characteristics in an embryo. Thus in the not too distant future it will be possible for parents to select some of their offspring's characteristics. And although many people would support the use of preimplantation genetic selection for couples who are carriers of a dreaded disease, many will not support this technology for couples who wish to have a child of a particular sex—or in the future, for a child with blue eyes, or musical talent, or who will be tall.

Preimplantation genetics, like many other technologies, raises the question of whether, because something can be done, it should be done. Many who believe in procreative liberty may extend that belief even further, asserting that people have a right to "select" the child they want to reproduce. Others, while still believing in the right to produce non-coitally, may see inherent dangers in society if couples are allowed to choose the characteristics of their offspring. The dilemma is where to draw the line—if anywhere—on this slippery high technological slope.

in the womb. This differs greatly from amniocentesis where fetal cells are nurtured in a culture solution and over days or weeks a large amount of material is generated, which is necessary to obtain dependable results. However, an embryo must be implanted in the womb soon after fertilization before it has divided too many times. The ability to test a single cell from an embryo is critical then, and technical advances in PGD eventually would allow it to be completed in less than twenty-four hours.

Scientists now know that removal of one or two cells from a four- or eight-cell embryo does not affect the ability of the embryo to continue growing or cause an abnormality. At this early stage, each cell is totipotent, that is, able to become a complete embryo by itself. Development is slowed slightly, but not adversely, so that the remaining cells will go on to form a complete, normal fetus. Also, almost without exception, the cells that are removed will have a genetic makeup identical to that of the remaining cells, making testing highly reliable.

The process of PGD starts as a typical IVF cycle. The ovaries are stimulated with hormonal injections and then anywhere from twelve to thirty eggs are retrieved. The eggs are placed in a petri dish along with sperm for fertilization. Three days later, around the eight-cell stage, the embryo is biopsied to remove one or two blastomeres (single cells) using micromanipulation techniques. This procedure, blastomere biopsy, was pioneered by three men at Cornell Medical College in New York—Zev Rosenwaks, James Grifo, and Santiago Munne—in the early 1990s.

First, the small cluster of cells that make up the embryo is steadied with a glass tube called a holding pipette while a tiny hole is made in the outer layer (zona pellucida) using a laser or an acid solution. Sometimes the opening is made instead by slicing with a sharp pipette. Then the blastomeres are carefully removed by gentle suction with a hollow glass needle and dissolved in a solution.

Small segments of DNA are selected and then amplified, or duplicated, millions of times using one of two techniques—polymerase chain reaction (PCR) or fluorescence in situ hybridization (FISH). Finally, with these large amounts of DNA available for examination, scientists can determine whether or not a genetic defect is present.

A Core Problem: Making Copies of DNA

What makes PGD practical, in fact, is the ability of technicians to make enough copies of a strand of DNA that is to be studied and to make those copies quickly. Speed is important, since the embryo needs to be implanted within 72 to 120 hours following the egg's retrieval.

Scientists had the ability to clone DNA, but this process took days and even weeks. Complicating matters was the fact that in order to study the DNA of a four- or eight-cell embryo, only one cell, two at most, would be available. Most scientists felt that PGD was not just unlikely but that it was impossible.

The enormity of the problem is explained by Lee M. Silver, author of *Remaking Eden*:

> Single cells carry only a single molecule of DNA with the instructions for each gene copy, and the difference between alleles [alternate forms of a gene] can be confined to just a dozen atoms. This means that if you want to know whether a particular allele is present in an embryo, you must have a technique that can distinguish whether a particular set of twelve atoms—hidden among the trillions of atoms that make up an embryonic cell—are present in one position or another. The technique must be rapid, accurate, cheap, and easy to perform on large numbers of samples.[30]

However, in 1983 the impossible became possible when biochemist Kary Mullis invented PCR. Because of Mullis's brainstorm, a single gene or DNA fragment can now be reproduced a million times in a matter of a few hours.

Creator of the Polymerase Chain Reaction (PCR)

It was a case of serendipity meets whimsy as Mullis got the notion one evening while steering his way along a California highway. "I was playing," he says. "I think really good science doesn't come from hard work. The striking advances come from people on the fringes, being playful." He related the moment in a 1993 interview with Jim Dwyer of the New York *Daily News* who wrote:

> How, he was pondering, could you find a single spot on the long, fragile DNA molecule? In a series of chemical acrobatic leaps, he realized that a section of DNA containing a gene or a fragment could be marked off, then forced into copying itself using replicating techniques similar to those DNA employs when a cell divides. Then he realized something so startling he had to pull the car to

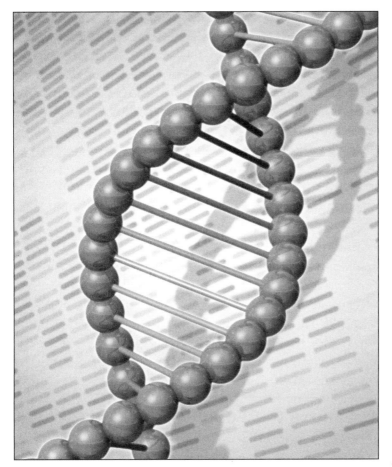

An illustration shows the double helix of a DNA strand. Doctors can determine physical traits and search for evidence of disease by examining an embryo's DNA.

the side of the road. When he had been messing with computer programs, he had been impressed by the power of a reiterative computer loop, in which the same process is repeated over and over. He saw how fast numbers can climb when they increase exponentially. Replicating DNA could work the same way: By adding the right chemicals, the little section of DNA could keep reproducing itself automatically and exponentially—so that the fragment would double, from two pieces, to four, to eight . . . and ever onward. In practical terms, he saw that, after eight doublings, he would have 256 copies of the gene. By the 20th cycle, he'd have 1,048,576. By the 30th, he'd be up to 1,073,741,824—a billion copies of a single gene in three hours. Bottomless vats of DNA, and easy to find.[31]

There are some who argue that Mullis was not the sole inventor of PCR but that it was the concerted effort of several scientists. The basis of their argument is that the concept of PCR alone was not sufficient; only when the technique was worked out and practiced in an experimental system did it become useful. Mullis himself admitted in a report to the Smithsonian Institution's Archive of Biotechnology that PCR was a concept rather than a specific technique. But to Mullis, making it work was second to dreaming up the idea. He says,

> The thing about PCR wasn't just putting those [things] together . . . the remarkable part is that you will pull out a little piece of DNA from its context, and that's what you will get amplified. . . . That was what I think of as the genius thing. . . . In a sense, I put together the elements that were already there. You can't make up new elements, usually. The new element, if any, was the combination, the way they were used. . . . The fact that I would do it over and over again, and the fact that I would do it in just the way I did, made it an invention.[32]

The Impact of PCR Technology

Thanks to PCR and the diagnostic tools it made possible, parents who are predisposed to genetic disease can obtain the peace of mind that comes from knowing that their children will be free of certain genetic defects. PCR has also been used in examining fetal DNA for different diseases, including the incompatibility of blood groups between mother and baby. With the advance warning that PCR detection provides, surgery can even be performed on a fetus to treat the problem.

While PCR has been a boon to couples with genetic concerns, the influence of PCR reaches far beyond the boundaries of reproductive technology. The ability to obtain rapid genetic profiles on humans—and plants and animals as well—has infiltrated agricultural and environmental science, criminal forensics, and molecular biology.

In the April 1990 issue of *Scientific American*, Mullis commented on the characteristics of PCR that make it so revolutionary:

> Beginning with a single molecule of the genetic material DNA, the PCR can generate 100 billion similar molecules in an afternoon. The reaction is easy to execute. It requires no more than a test tube, a few simple reagents, and a source of heat. The DNA sample that one wishes to copy can be pure, or it can be a minute part of an extremely complex mixture of biological materials. The DNA may come from a hospital tissue specimen, from a single human hair, from a drop of dried blood at the scene of a crime, from the tissues of a mummified brain, or from a 40,000-year-old wooly mammoth frozen in a glacier.[33]

Fluorescent In Situ Hybridization (FISH)

PCR became the standard technique involved in identifying problems that are the result of single-gene

Technology and PCR

According to the website Breakthroughs in Bioscience, the equipment used for PCR is destined to become smaller and easier to use as the technology continues to improve.

The technology for doing PCR—about the size of a microwave oven and costing several thousand dollars—seems destined for further radical improvement. By tinkering with variables such as chemical reagents and pH, researchers have already reported success at copying larger and larger pieces of DNA, including the entire genome of HIV.

Extraordinary miniaturization of the hardware is also underway, as experimenters squeeze PCR onto chip-sized devices. Crisscrossed with the tiniest troughs to hold the reagents and the DNA, the chips are heated electrically and cool down much faster than the present generation of machines, so amplification is even speedier than the already swift process. And researchers have reported using a handheld, battery-powered gadget to copy pieces of DNA that contained eight different cystic fibrosis mutation sites.

While such experimental, chip-based devices were not ready for prime time as the twenty-first century opened, they are hastening the day when scientists can take them on the road and patients will be able to get on-the-spot readouts of their DNA. Before long it may be quite routine to diagnose an infectious or genetic disorder, or even detect an inherited predisposition to cancer or heart disease, right in the doctor's office.

defects, including cystic fibrosis, sickle-cell anemia, Tay-Sachs disease, and Huntington's disease. However, PCR is not effective in assessing chromosomal defects such as abnormalities caused by three copies of a chromosome rather than two, for example, Down syndrome (chromosome 21), Edward's syndrome (chromosome 18), and Patau's syndrome (chromosome 13). While it can detect the X or Y chromosome, it cannot tell the number of copies in the target sequence of DNA, which is needed when determining a chromosome abnormality.

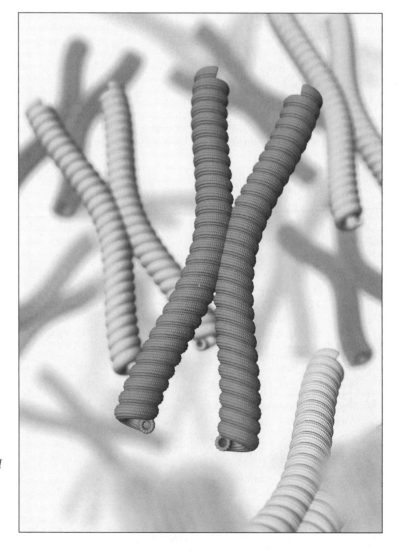

Computer artwork shows normal human chromosomes. Deformed chromosomes can cause conditions such as Down syndrome and cystic fibrosis.

A second technique for performing PGD is FISH. Most commonly used for chromosomal analysis, it detects chromosomes in their normal place in the nucleus (*in situ* is Latin for "at the site"). Lab workers add single strands of DNA that have been modified to glow in different colors, and that will bind to certain chromosomes. The copies of each chromosome will glow in the specific color, allowing them to be counted and thus screened for abnormality. The one disadvantage of FISH is that only a handful of chromosomes can be tested at one time. The limitation is the number of different colors that can be observed in the same viewing.

The Future of PGD

The place of PGD in the history of reproductive technology cannot be underestimated. Like the other techniques used to help ease the problem of infertility, it has made a difference in the lives of millions of people. Couples who might have remained childless out of fear of passing along genetic defects now have an option. However, as Brian Kearney warns, along with the technology comes a responsibility to use it wisely. Many of the choices made by reproductive specialists and their patients involve controversial issues that lack simple resolutions.

> PGD is still in its infancy, but it is developing quickly. Like other technologies developed as part of reproductive medicine, it offers great promise of reducing suffering, but it brings with it important social and ethical implications as well. As the technology becomes more powerul, it will reach into the lives of more people, and its implications will have to be faced.[34]

CHAPTER 6

Drawing the Line: Ethical, Moral, and Social Questions

The variety of assisted reproductive technologies (ART) available at the opening of the twenty-first century have helped more than half a million infertile couples in the United States alone become parents. Yet this plethora of choices results in ethical, moral, and social debates. Supporters of reproductive technology cite obvious benefits, while opponents strongly criticize it for lacking respect for human life. Because something *can* be done, they ask, *should* it be done?

Modern science has forced doctors and patients to face this difficult question, as noted by Cooper and Glazer.

> [Today's infertile] couples travel a very different journey than their counterparts from any prior generation. Even recent generations had few medical interventions to which they could turn. In contrast, today's weary travelers make their way through a complex and confusing medical maze . . . many find themselves approaching the unfamiliar ter-

rain of the assisted reproductive technologies. This terrain may necessitate difficult, complicated, and ethically challenging decisions that may even involve third or fourth parties in the parenting experience.[35]

The Fate of Frozen Embryos

Central to many debates over reproductive technology is the philosophical question of what constitutes a person. This issue is of particular importance when a decision has to be made about the fate of frozen embryos. A normal IVF cycle can generate anywhere from one dozen to nearly three dozen eggs for fertilization. A few of the resulting embryos are implanted and, under procedures at most IVF clinics by the early twenty-first century, the remainder are cryopreserved. Freezing embryos allows the couple to repeat an IVF cycle but without the stress of hormonal stimulation and egg retrieval. Furthermore, since this is the most expensive part of the process, eliminating this step is also cost-effective for the patient. But a couple will more than likely never use all their embryos, even if they go through several cycles of IVF.

What, then, the ethicists and others ask, is to be done with all those extra embryos? If the embryos are disposed of, is a life being destroyed? Some argue that the eight-celled embryo is not a life at that point but merely holds the *potential* for life, given the right environment. Others say that a life begins at conception and that to treat the embryo as anything else is immoral. Pam Madsen, executive director of the American Infertility Association said, "Some people just can't cope with the decision. Even though their religious or moral perspectives about when life begins are all very individual and different, still most of them will agree that their embryos are very special."[36]

One way people have avoided making a decision on the issue is to keep their frozen embryos indefinitely. While embryo storage may seem like an acceptable solution, it has created a host of questions. One that arises is how long IVF clinics should be obligated to store the

The Definition of Mother

Susan Lewis Cooper and Ellen Sarasohn Glazer, authors of Choosing Assisted Reproduction: Social, Emotional, and Ethical Considerations, *discuss how assisted reproduction has complicated the use of the word* mother.

Traditionally, motherhood and gestation have been linked, so that the notion of genetics seemed incidental. However, over the years we have come to understand the importance of genetics in shaping a person's life. Although it is impossible to separate the exact roles that nature and nurture play in one's life, all agree that each is important in creating the adult. The genetic mother—the ovum donor—is therefore extremely important to the child's identity, regardless of whether she donates anonymously or is known to the parents. Those who question the ethics of intentionally separating the genetic and gestational aspect of motherhood believe that it is not in the child's best interest to be deliberately brought into the world surrounded by this confusion.

Although the new definitions of mother are easily understandable, even to those not involved in reproductive technology, in the legal sense they can be baffling. Many argue that the woman who delivers a child should legally be considered the "real" mother, unless or until she gives up her rights to rear the child. Those who argue this point believe that even in situations in which a gestational carrier is used, she is the "real" mother despite the fact that her gamete was not used in creating the child. Others argue that the genetic mother is the "real" mother, regardless of whether she carries the baby.

Reproductive technologies have forever altered the traditional meaning of motherhood.

frozen embryos. In Britain, for example, there is a five-year maximum imposed by the government. On the other hand, the United States has no such time limit. As a result, according to a report released by the Society for Assisted Reproductive Technology in May 2003, an estimated four hundred thousand embryos are suspended in cryotanks in IVF clinics across the country—the largest population of frozen embryos in the world.

Some experts, like Douglas Melton, a Harvard University researcher, see the long-term storage as wasteful, saying "These embryos could be put to a number of good research purposes."[37] The aim of such research, for example, would be to learn how to prevent birth defects and how to cure various disorders such as Alzheimer's disease or Parkinson's disease.

Paul Lauritzen, director of the applied ethics program at John Carroll University in Cleveland, Ohio, decries the way the debate is characterized by extreme views at either end of the spectrum. He writes: "[People believe that] either the fetus is a person with a full set of rights, or it is nothing but a clump of cells with little or no moral claim on us all. . . . If we are to think and speak truthfully about embryo research, we must repudiate the extremes and find a middle ground."[38]

The debate over an embryo's status has found its way into court. In a 1994 case, for example, a couple going through a divorce asked a court to decide whether their stored embryos were property to be divided in the settlement. The wife wanted to keep them for later implantation, even though she would no longer be married to the father. The husband wanted them destroyed. The court eventually decided in favor of the wife; however, by that time, she had remarried and decided to donate the embryos to another infertile couple.

The Commercialization of Sperm, Eggs, and Embryos

For some, viewing embryos as property opens the possibility of selling them. Indeed, the sale of eggs and sperm has already occurred. "The demand is increasing for human eggs," says Jeffrey P. Kahn, director of the Center for Bioethics at the University of Minnesota. "But donated eggs still remain a scarce commodity, and as the price being paid to donors rises well into the thousands of dollars (average price in New York City is reportedly $5,000 per donation and rising), it is time to ask whether we've created a market in human eggs."[39]

Some ethicists say that eggs and sperm should be looked at in the same way as body parts, such as kidneys. That is, they should be available to those who need them but not be sold to the highest bidder. Kahn, for one, argues that donors of eggs should be only modestly compensated at most:

> The closest we should come to a market for eggs or organs is to provide reimbursement for the costs associated with the donation, such as payment for lost wages and transportation; and at most provide a standard and consistent monetary standard to encourage altruism. We should not be paying donors to ignore or overlook the risks of their donation, and the higher the pay the more likely that is to happen. The resulting donations should not be allocated based on market forces but distributed according to medical need and waiting time. If we choose another course, the price to be paid by commodifying human body parts is even higher than the price of organ shortage.[40]

Despite ethical misgivings eggs, and even embryos, are being purchased. In her book *The Clone Age: Adventures in the New World of Reproductive Technology*, author and attorney Lori B. Andrews describes one medical center where an embryo can be created to order. For a little less than three thousand dollars, a couple can obtain an embryo made from donor sperm and eggs, both chosen by the couple based on traits of the donors.

Such a practice troubles Andrews, who notes a trend toward trait selection by couples. Andrews questions how even less sophisticated technologies, such as DI, are being applied: "Making a baby is starting to resemble buying a car, with choices galore about which features and extras to request. Each year, thousands of births occur through donor insemination, with many people choosing their future children based on the hair color, height, weight, and SAT scores of a donor."[41]

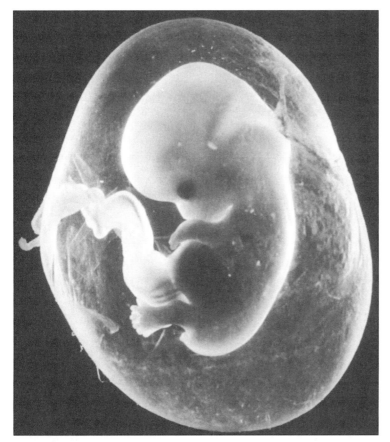

There are many ethical concerns surrounding genetic manipulation. Many fear the technology could be used to create custom-made babies.

Designer Children

Technologies such as PGD trouble those who foresee a time when these advanced procedures will go beyond the prevention of congenital defects and be used in the creation of so-called designer babies. While some experts see this phenomenon as being far in the future, they predict an explosive impact when it does arrive. M. Crenson, a writer for the Associated Press, has this to say about the future of genetic manipulation: "Most researchers believe it will be decades before doctors slip genes into human beings as easily as we load programs onto home computers today from CD-ROMs. But when they do, the sky will be the limit."[42]

Beyond the concerns about the ethics of genetic manipulation, some observers are opposed to such

Sperm as a Commodity

Sperm donors receive considerably less money (fifty dollars per vial) than egg donors, but sperm is easier to obtain. Egg donors endure ovarian stimulation and egg retrieval surgery, investing more time and physical risk than sperm donors. Another difference is that while the technology for freezing eggs has not been fully developed yet, the capability for freezing sperm has existed for several decades. Douglas Frank, in his article appearing in *Rutgers Focus*, "The Venerable Sperm: A Crisis of Identity in the Modern Age," quotes historians Janet Golden and Cynthia Daniels as noting, "the practice of selling sperm has discovered the Internet. As a commodity on the open market, sperm is now priced online at about $165 for a specimen. Semen can be sent by Federal Express and credit cards are accepted." However, Golden and Daniels do not recommend this source of sperm, as it represents an underground market where donors have probably not been medically screened.

research because they believe it will lead to a policy of discrimination based on genetic traits. Michael S. Langan, vice president of the National Organization for Rare Disorders, Inc., argues: "There will be many wealthy people willing and eager to pay the price of making their child taller and more beautiful. Eventually there will be discrimination against those who look 'different' because their genes were *not* altered."[43]

Silver has a more optimistic view of the power of genetic enhancement. He suggests,

> Why not seize the power? Why not control what has been left to chance in the past? Indeed, we control all other aspects of our children's lives and identities through powerful social and environmental influences and, in some cases, with the use of powerful drugs like Ritalin or Prozac. On what basis can we reject positive genetic influences on a person's essence when we accept the rights of parents to benefit their children in every other way?[44]

Does IVF Damage Babies' Genes?

Another aspect of the debate over reproductive technology is the ongoing question over how safe the procedures are for the children produced by them. For example, one concern that has surfaced is whether babies created via IVF have an increased risk of birth defects. Several studies done in 2002 have linked IVF and ICSI (intracytoplasmic sperm injection) with a higher risk for birth defects, such as heart and kidney abnormalities and cleft palate, a rare type of eye cancer, and lower birth weight.

Reproductive technology has helped countless infertile couples. How safe the technologies are for the children created by them, however, is a hotly debated issue.

There is much speculation about possible causes. One theory is that the culture medium used in the lab for supporting eggs and embryos until implantation has something to do with the problem. Two researchers at the University of Pennsylvania believe that variations in amounts of salt or amino acids used in the culture solution may be prompting the genes involved to turn on when they should be off and vice versa.

Most infertile couples, however, are willing to overlook the increased risks in hopes of having a baby. Zev Rosenwaks, director of New York–Presbyterian Hospital's infertility program explains, "If you ask a couple if they would rather not have a child at all or try to have a child that over 90% of the time will be normal, I think they will choose to have the child."[45]

Risks Associated with Fertility Drugs and Multiple Births

The risks reproductive technologies pose for the children are only beginning to be studied. More thoroughly researched and documented are the risks faced by the women who make use of reproductive technologies. For example, fertility drugs used to induce superovulation are powerful, and it is impossible to predict how an individual woman's ovaries will react to them. Some women will experience swelling and bleeding of the ovaries, fluid retention, and in extreme cases, heart failure. Furthermore, egg retrieval and embryo implantation are both invasive procedures; a needle is inserted through the vaginal wall to collect eggs from the ovary, and the embryo is sometimes returned deep into the fallopian tubes. In addition, several inconclusive studies leave open the possibility that women who take fertility drugs face an increased risk of ovarian cancer.

Another controversy raised by IVF is how to handle the multiple fetuses that often result from the procedure. To increase the chances of success, doctors will usually transfer several embryos. However, the risks to

both mother and the children when multiple embryos implant are well documented. If a number of embryos do implant, parents are faced with a dilemma: reduce the number of fetuses by aborting some or carry on with the multiple-fetus pregnancy. In her book, *The Clone Age,* Lori B. Andrews notes one example:

> Bobbi McCaughey [mother of septuplets born in 1997 and conceived with the help of fertility drugs] was, of course, offered the option of "selectively reducing" some of her seven offspring. Doctors were shocked when she refused because of her deeply felt religious beliefs. Yet it is perfectly understandable that an infertile woman could find it emotionally wrenching to terminate lives she and her husband worked so hard to create. [46]

Some doctors refuse to implant more than two or three embryos because of the risks to the fetuses' development

One risk of in vitro fertilization is multiple births. Bobbi McCaughey gave birth to septuplets in 1997.

in multiple births. Britain has even enacted a law prohibiting doctors there from transferring more than three embryos per IVF procedure. In the United States there are no such laws, but the American Society for Reproductive Medicine recommends that no more than three be implanted.

How Old Is Too Old?

IVF and related technologies even raise the question of *who* should become a parent. For example, even when a woman is past menopause, it is possible for her to become pregnant through the use of donor eggs and hormone therapy to stimulate her aging reproductive system. Critics of such a practice claim that women in their fifties and sixties are not fit to meet the heavy demands of parenting. Ana Veciana-Suarez, a reporter for Knight-Ridder/Tribune News Service, explains her position:

> Nature knew what it was doing when it set its own cut-off date for child-bearing. It wasn't trying to be arbitrary, just logical. Natural evolution protects us from ourselves, whether or not we understand or like it. An older woman's body cannot handle the strains of pregnancy as well as when she was younger, nor can she handle the long, arduous labor of raising a child.[47]

Those in favor of offering reproductive technologies to such women decry such a double standard, noting that men in their sixties and beyond can and do father children. These advocates also cite the rights of individuals to make reproductive choices regardless of what others might say. They believe that as long as a woman is emotionally and physically healthy, there is no reason why age should be a barrier any more than it is for men.

The Need for Regulation

Some countries have attempted to use legislation to address some questions, although the U.S. government has been reluctant to do so. The result of this hands-off policy is an industry that is self-regulated or, as some observers see it, unregulated. Francine Kiefer, writer for the *Christian Science Monitor*, asserts, "Largely unregulated, the [fertility] clinics are an exception in medicine. In them, scientific application goes directly from animal testing to widespread human use—skipping the human trial and oversight phases. This not only raises questions of medical risk, but also profound ethical issues."[48]

Some who recoil at the idea of the government regulation see at least some self-regulation as necessary—if only to forestall the much less palatable alternative. As the technology has developed over the last decade, particularly in the area of genetic manipulation, and with cloning of humans looming on the horizon, attempts have been made to ban such procedures. "The more the profession doesn't regulate itself, the more it's really taking a risk of having something externally imposed," says Rebecca Dresser, professor of law and ethics at Washington University in St. Louis, Missouri. "The more we hear about disturbing practices, the more that risk increases."[49]

In 1992 the government did enact the Fertility Clinic Success Rate and Certification Act that requires clinics to keep and report success statistics. "But," according to Shannon Brownlee, editor at *U.S. News & World Report*, "the minimal oversight will do little to improve the success rates at the worst clinics, leaving it to couples to separate the truth from the hype. In the worst cases, they run up huge bills in repeated and futile attempts to get pregnant."[50]

Geoffrey Sher says the time is now to move away from inconsistently applied recommendations and guidelines that are ineffectual and that open the industry to abuse. He believes the most responsible action would be to have directives come from the national level but only after input and consensus from a variety of interest

IVF Technology and Human Cloning?

Gina Kolata, author of Clone: The Road to Dolly and the Path Ahead, *discusses the connection between IVF technology and human cloning. Without the ability to manipulate sperm and egg, cloning would not be possible. But the ethics of creating a child from the genes of its mother and father may differ from the ethics of creating a child who is the exact genetic copy of another person.*

If there is one lesson of cloning it is that there is no uniformly accepted way to think about the ethical questions that it elicits, and no agreement, even among the most thoughtful and well-informed commentators, about what is right and what is wrong. Many—but by no means all—theologians tend to condemn the notion of human cloning. Many ethicists were similarly repelled, but others asked instead, who would be harmed, and why are we so sure that harm would ensue? While theologians cited religious traditions and biblical proscriptions, lawyers cited reproductive rights and said it would be very hard to argue that it was illegal to clone oneself. In the meantime, some ethicists said they'd heard from in vitro clinics, which—operating already outside the usual rules that bind scientists, and looking for paying customers—were extremely interested in investigating cloning.

groups: consumers, physicians, IVF doctors, clergy, fertility support groups, ethicists, insurance companies, and legislators. He argues:

> For the thousands of couples whose lives have been enriched by the gift of life through IVF and other assisted reproductive technologies, for the many more infertile couples who have little hope of conceiving without the assistance of these procedures, and mindful of the sacred doctrine that obliges the medical profession to improve the human condition and alleviate suffering wherever possible, we challenge the medical/scientific communities and consumers alike to strive together to expand the technology, improve the quality, and promote the affordability and accessibility of IVF and related technologies.[51]

The debate over reproductive technologies shows little sign of dying down. Ronald Bailey, science correspondent for *Reason* magazine, claims that medical issues like this one will always have two sides. "Where many see steady incremental progress toward healing more and more human ills," Bailey says, "others see a slippery slope down which a hapless humanity is uncontrollably sliding."[52]

The long-held beliefs of what makes a parent and how children are conceived and born have been challenged. Now, at the opening of the twenty-first century, ongoing research in reproductive technology simply promises that the debate will continue.

NOTES

Introduction: Reproductive Technology: New Hope for Infertile Couples

1. Lynda Beck Fenwick, *Private Choices, Public Consequences.* New York: Dutton, 1998, p. 255.
2. Gina Kolata, *Clone: The Road to Dolly and the Path Ahead.* New York: William Morrow, 1998, p. 13.
3. Brian Kearney, *High-Tech Conception: A Comprehensive Handbook for Consumers.* New York: Bantam Books, 1998, p. xiii.

Chapter 1: Treating Male Infertility: Artificial and Donor Insemination

4. Susan Lewis Cooper and Ellen Sarasohn Glazer, *Choosing Assisted Reproduction: Social, Emotional, and Ethical Considerations.* Indianapolis: Perspective Press, 1998, p. 152.
5. Gina Maranto, *Quest for Perfection: The Drive to Breed Better Human Beings.* New York: Simon & Schuster, 1996, p. 154.
6. Maranto, *Quest for Perfection*, p. 162.
7. Maranto, *Quest for Perfection*, p. 154.
8. Lee M. Silver, *Remaking Eden: Cloning and Beyond in a Brave New World.* New York: Avon Books, 1997, p. 153.
9. Maranto, *Quest for Perfection*, p. 156.
10. Cooper and Glazer, *Choosing Assisted Reproduction*, p. 184.

11. Quoted in Carol Wekesser, ed., *Reproductive Technologies.* San Diego: Greenhaven Press, 1995, p. 18.

Chapter 2: Fertility Enhancement: Drug Therapy and Microsurgery

12. Sherman J. Silber, *How to Get Pregnant with the New Technology.* New York: Warner Books, 1991, p. 197.
13. Gary S. Berger, Marc Goldstein, and Mark Fuerst, *The Couple's Guide to Fertility.* New York: Doubleday, 1995, p. 161.
14. Carla Harkness, *The Infertility Book: A Comprehensive Medical and Emotional Guide.* Berkeley, CA: Celestial Arts, 1992, p. 144.
15. Maranto, *Quest for Perfection,* p. 204.

Chapter 3: The Keystone of Assisted Reproduction: In Vitro Fertilization

16. Quoted in Maranto, *Quest for Perfection,* p. 196.
17. Quoted in Maranto, *Quest for Perfection,* p. 197.
18. Maranto, *Quest for Perfection,* p. 201
19. Silver, *Remaking Eden,* p. 68.
20. Silver, *Remaking Eden,* p. 68.

Chapter 4: Surrogacy, Egg Donation, and Embryo Adoption

21. Geoffrey Sher, Virginia Marriage Davis, and Jean Stoess, *In Vitro Fertilization: The A.R.T. of Making Babies.* NewYork: Facts On File, 1998, p. 155.
22. Thomas M. Pinkerton, "Surrogacy and Egg Donation Law in California," The American Surrogacy Center, March 2001. www.surrogacy.com.
23. Quoted in Sher, Davis, and Stoess, *In Vitro Fertilization,* p. 167.
24. Quoted in *Omaha World Herald,* "Woman Gives Birth to Her Own Grandkids," October 20, 2002.
25. Quoted in Anita Hamilton, "Eggs on Ice," *Time,* July 1, 2002, p. 55.
26. Cooper and Glazer, *Choosing Assisted Reproduction,* pp. 331–32.

Chapter 5: Preventing Inherited Disease: Preimplantation Genetic Diagnosis

27. HELP—Health Education Library for People, "Using PGD to Prevent Sex-Linked Diseases," 2003. www.healthlibrary.com.
28. Maranto, *Quest for Perfection,* p. 267.
29. James Trefil, "Brave New World," *Smithsonian,* December 2001.
30. Silver, *Remaking Eden,* p. 204.
31. Jim Dwyer, "The Quirky Genius Who Is Changing Our Lives," University of Kentucky, 2003. www.uky.edu.
32. Quoted in Paul Rabinow, "What is PCR?" Sun SITE, 1998, http://sunsite.berkeley.edu.
33. Quoted in Kary Mullis, "Polymerase Chain Reaction," Kary Mullis, 2002. www.karymullis.com.
34. Kearney, *High-Tech Conception,* p. 317.

Chapter 6: Drawing the Line: Ethical, Moral, and Social Questions

35. Cooper and Glazer, *Choosing Assisted Reproduction,* p. 14.
36. Quoted in Rick Weiss, "400,000 Embryos Frozen in U.S.," *Washington Post,* May 8, 2003. www.washingtonpost.com.
37. Quoted in Weiss, "400,000 Embryos Frozen in U.S."
38. Paul Lauritzen, "Neither Person Nor Property: Embryo Research and the Status of the Early Embryo," *America,* March 26, 2001. www.americamagazine.org.
39. Jeffrey P. Kahn, "Is There a Difference Between Selling Eggs and Selling Kidneys?" CNN Interactive, May 1998. www.cnn.com.
40. Kahn, "Is There a Difference Between Selling Eggs and Selling Kidneys?"
41. Lori B. Andrews, "Designer Babies," *Reader's Digest,* July 2001.
42. M. Crenson, "New Science May Give Parents Some Control over Children's Genes," *Athens Banner-Herald,* January 19, 2003. www.onlineathens.com.
43. Quoted in Rick Weiss, "Gene Enhancements' Thorny

Ethical Traits: Rapid Fire Discoveries Force Examination of Consequences," *Washington Post,* October 12, 1997, n.p.

44. Silver, *Remaking Eden,* p. 236.

45. Quoted in Michael D. Lemonick, "Risky Business?" *Time,* March 18, 2002.

46. Lori B. Andrews, *The Clone Age: Adventures in the New World of Reproductive Technology.* New York: Henry Holt, 1999, p. 57.

47. Ana Veciana-Suarez, "Postmenopausal Women Should Not Become Pregnant," in Wekesser, *Reproductive Technologies,* p. 67.

48. Francine Kiefer, "A Call for Federal Oversight of Fertility Clinics," *Christian Science Monitor,* August 21, 2001. www.csmonitor.com.

49. Quoted in Vida Foubister, "Reproductive Technologies Outpacing Ethical Consideration," *American Medical News,* January 17, 2000, American Medical Association. www.ama-assn.org.

50. Shannon Brownlee, "Regulation of Reproductive Technologies: An Overview," in Wekesser, *Reproductive Technologies,* p. 151.

51. Sher, Davis, and Stoess, *In Vitro Fertilization,* p. 193.

52. Ronald Bailey, "Techno Baby Steps," *Reason,* May 23, 2001. http://reason.com.

FOR FURTHER READING

Michelle Arnot, *101 Answers to Your Fertility Questions.* New York: Dell, 1997. A general guidebook to infertility causes and treatments.

Ann Fullick, *Test Tube Babies: In Vitro Fertilization.* Heinemann Library, 2002. A book for younger readers on IVF.

Kenny McCaughey and Bobbi McCaughey, *Seven from Heaven: The Miracle of the McCaughey Septuplets.* Nashville: Thomas Nelson, 1998. Outlines the before-and-after story of the famous McCaughey septuplets.

Tamra B. Orr, *Test Tube Babies.* Blackbirch Press, 2003. Basic information about IVF for middle-school students.

Alistair G. Sutcliffe, *IVF Children: The First Generation.* New York: Parthenon, 2002. Reviews current knowledge about the physical and mental effects on children born following cryopreservation, ICSI, and other IVF techniques.

Carol Wekesser, ed., *Reproductive Technologies.* San Diego: Greenhaven Press, 1995. A collection of articles from magazines and newspapers, and excerpts from books and speeches, that express varying opinions on ART.

WORKS CONSULTED

Books

Lori B. Andrews, *The Clone Age: Adventures in the New World of Reproductive Technology*. New York: Henry Holt, 1999. An overview of the legal and ethical aspects of surrogate motherhood, cloning, artificial insemination, and IVF-related genetics.

Gary S. Berger, Marc Goldstein, and Mark Fuerst, *The Couple's Guide to Fertility*. New York: Doubleday, 1995. Surveys all the options available to couples, including fertility drugs, surrogacy, IVF, and sperm and egg donation.

Susan Lewis Cooper and Ellen Sarasohn Glazer, *Choosing Assisted Reproduction: Social, Emotional, and Ethical Considerations*. Indianapolis: Perspective Press, 1998. Details the medical, legal, ethical, and psychological implications of ART.

C. Maud Doherty and Melanie Morrissey Clark, *The Fertility Handbook: A Guide to Getting Pregnant*. Omaha, NE: Addicus Books, 2002. Presents basic information to infertility patients about various ART procedures.

Robert Edwards and Patrick Steptoe, *A Matter of Life: The Story of a Medical Breakthrough*. New York: William Morrow, 1980. Details from the authors about their achievement as the first to make a test-tube baby.

Lynda Beck Fenwick, *Private Choices, Public Consequences*. New York: Dutton, 1998. Explores the complex issues surrounding ART and includes many stories from people and the experts involved with them.

Carla Harkness, *The Infertility Book: A Comprehensive Medical and Emotional Guide.* Berkeley, CA: Celestial Arts, 1992. Provides helpful information on fertility, and detailed explanations of medical procedures.

Brian Kearney, *High-Tech Conception: A Comprehensive Handbook for Consumers.* New York: Bantam Books, 1998. Outlines the risks and benefits of various IVF techniques and also offers advice on selecting a fertility doctor and clinic.

Gina Kolata, *Clone: The Road to Dolly and the Path Ahead.* New York: William Morrow, 1998. Tells the story behind the development of cloning and what the technology may hold for humans.

Gina Maranto, *Quest for Perfection: The Drive to Breed Better Human Beings.* New York: Simon & Schuster, 1996. A comprehensive social history from the early history of childbearing through the new reproductive technologies.

M. Sara Rosenthal, *The Fertility Sourcebook.* Los Angeles: Lowell House, 1996. Helps consumers make informed choices by providing complete and clear information about all aspects of infertility.

Geoffrey Sher, Virginia Marriage Davis, and Jean Stoess, *In Vitro Fertilization: The A.R.T. of Making Babies.* New York: Facts On File, 1998. Well-written handbook covering not only the physical aspects of fertility treatment but the emotional, financial, and ethical issues as well.

David Shier, Jackie Butler, and Ricki Lewis. *Hole's Human Anatomy and Physiology,* 9th ed. New York: McGraw Hill, 2002. Textbook for high school and college-level science students.

Sherman J. Silber, *How to Get Pregnant with the New Technology.* New York: Warner Books, 1991. A good resource for infertility patients.

Lee M. Silver, *Remaking Eden: Cloning and Beyond in a Brave New World.* New York: Avon Books, 1997. Offers an optimistic viewpoint on the benefits of genetic engineering.

Periodicals

Lori B. Andrews, "Designer Babies," *Reader's Digest*, July 2001.

Christine Gorman, "The Limits of Science," *Time*, April 15, 2002.

Anita Hamilton, "Eggs on Ice," *Time*, July 1, 2002.

Gabor T. Kovacs, Sue A. Breheny, and Melinda J. Dear, "Embryo Donation at an Australian University In-Vitro Fertilisation Clinic: Issues and Outcomes," *Medical Journal of Australia*, February 3, 2003.

Michael D. Lemonick, "Risky Business?" *Time*, March 18, 2002.

Omaha World Herald, "Clinics Pay Big Bucks to Student Egg Donors," May 24, 2003.

———, "Some GIs Banking Fatherhood Insurance Before They Go," January 30, 2003.

———, "Woman Gives Birth to Own Grandkids," October 20, 2002.

Elizabeth Hervey Stephen, "Assisted Reproductive Technologies: Is the Price Too High?" *Population Today*, May 1999.

James Trefil, "Brave New World," *Smithsonian*, December 2001.

James D. Watson, "Moving Toward Clonal Man: Is This What We Want?" *Atlantic Monthly*, May 1971.

Rick Weiss, "Gene Enhancements' Thorny Ethical Traits: Rapid-Fire Discoveries Force Examination of Consequences," *Washington Post*, October 12, 1997.

Internet Sources

American Society for Reproductive Medicine, "Posthumous Reproduction," 2000–2002. www.asrm.org.

———, "A Practice Committee Report: Preimplantation Genetic Diagnosis," 2001. www.asrm.org.

American Surrogacy Center, "Legal Overview of Surrogacy Laws by State," March 1997. http://surrogacy.com.

Ronald Bailey, "Techno Baby Steps," *Reason*, May 23, 2001. http://reason.com.

Seymour Brody, "Dr. Gregory Goodwin Pincus: Father of 'The Pill,'" Florida Atlantic University, 2002. www.fau.edu.

California Cryobank, "History of Sperm Banking," 1993. www.cryobank.com.

Carolina Biological Supply Company, "Great Achievements in Science: Kary Mullis," 2003. www.carolina.com.

R. Alta Charo, "Children by Choice: Reproductive Technologies and the Boundaries of Personal Autonomy," *Nature*, October 1, 2002. www.nature.com.

Chicago-Kent College of Law, Illinois Institute of Technology, "The Laws of Reproductive Technology," 2002–2003. www.kentlaw.edu.

———, "State Laws on Surrogacy—Table IV," 2002–2003. www.kentlaw.edu.

Columbia Encyclopedia, 5th ed., "Bayliss, Sir William Maddock," Columbia University Press, 1995, Slider. www.slider.com.

M. Crenson, "New Science May Give Parents Some Control over Children's Genes," *Athens Banner-Herald*, January 19, 2003. www.onlineathens.com.

Jessica Dunsmore, "Economics of Technology," May 3, 2003, Wellesley College. www.wellesley.edu.

Jim Dwyer, "The Quirky Genius Who Is Changing Our Lives," University of Kentucky, 2003. www.uky.edu.

Endocrine Society, "History of Endocrinology," 2003. www.endo-society.org.

Vida Foubister, "Reproductive Technologies Outpacing Ethical Consideration," *American Medical News*, January 17, 2000, American Medical Association. www.ama-assn.org.

Douglas Frank, "The Venerable Sperm: A Crisis of Identity in the Modern Age," *Rutgers Focus*, March 3, 2000, Rutgers, The State University of New Jersey. http://uc.rutgers.edu.

Gale Group, "In the Matter of Baby M: 1998." www.galegroup.com.

Donald I. Galen, "Advances in Microsurgery for Female Infertility," Reproductive Science Center of the San Francisco Bay Area, 2000–2002. www.drgalen.com.

Genesis IVF, "Learn About IVF," 2002. www.genesisivf.com.

Genetics and IVF Institute, "Preimplantation Genetic Diagnosis," 2003. www.givf.com.

Roy O. Greep, "Min Chueh Chang," in *Biographical Memoirs*, vol. 68, National Academy of Sciences, 1996, National Academies Press. www.nap.edu.

HELP—Health Education Library for People, "Using PGD to Prevent Sex-Linked Diseases," 2003. www.health library.com.

Huntington Reproductive Center, "Artificial Insemination (AI)/Intrauterine Insemination (IUI)/Gender Selection," 2003. www.havingbabies.com.

IntegraMed America, "Preimplantation Diagnosis," 2003. www.integramed.com.

Jeffrey P. Kahn, "Is There a Difference Between Selling Eggs and Selling Kidneys?" CNN Interactive, May 1998. www.cnn.com.

Francine Kiefer, "A Call for Federal Oversight of Fertility Clinics," *Christian Science Monitor*, August 21, 2001. www.csmonitor.com.

Lasker Foundation, "Albert Lasker Award for Clinical Medical Research, 2001." www.laskerfoundation.org.

Paul Lauritzen, "Neither Person Nor Property: Embryo Research and the Status of the Early Embryo," *America*, March 26, 2001. www.americamagazine.org.

Julie Severens Lyons, "Artificial Wombs Could Take Pregnancy into Laboratory," *Mercury News*, February 23, 2002, Silicon Valley. www.siliconvally.com.

Monash IVF Australia, "Key Milestones at Monash IVF," 1999. www.monashivf.edu.au.

Kary Mullis, "Polymerase Chain Reaction," Kary Mullis, 2002. www.karymullis.com.

National Conference of Commissioners on Uniform State Laws, "The Uniform Parentage Act 2000," American

Academy of Matrimonial Lawyers, 2000. www. aaml.org.

Thomas M. Pinkerton, "Surrogacy and Egg Donation Law in California," The American Surrogacy Center, March 2001. www.surrogacy.com.

Tabitha M. Powledge, "The Polymerase Chain Reaction," Breakthroughs in Bioscience—Federation of American Societies for Experimental Biology, 2003. www.faseb.org.

PregnancyMD, "Tubal Disease and Microsurgery," 2001. www.pregnancymd.org.

Paul Rabinow, "What is PCR?" Sun SITE, 1998. http://sun site.berkeley.edu.

Reproductive Science Center of the San Francisco Bay Area, "Microsurgery for Female Infertility," 1999–2002. www.rscbayarea.com.

Sher Institute for Reproductive Medicine, "Therapeutic Reproductive Surgery," 1999–2002. www.haveababy. com.

Society for Reproduction and Fertility, "F.H.A. Marshall Biography." www.srf-reproduction.org.

Stephen Smith, "The Fertility Race, Part Seven, Twenty Years of Test-Tube Babies," MPR, 1998. http://news. mpr.org.

———, "Sir Alan Parkes Biography," 2003. www.srf-repro duction.org.

Timelinescience, "Infertility Treatment Timeline," 2002. www.timelinescience.org.

———, "Treating Infertility with IVF," 2002. www.time linescience.org.

21st Century Medicine, "Origins of Cryobiology," 1999–2001. www.21cm.com.

Vorzimer, Masserman, and Chapman, "In Vitro Fertilization and the Law: Gestational Surrogacy," 1997. www.vg me.com.

Rick Weiss, "400,000 Embryos Frozen in U.S.," *Washington Post*, May 8, 2003. www.washingtonpost.com.

Westside Pregnancy Resource Center, "Japanese Scientist Develops Artificial Womb," Reuters, July 1997. www.w-cpc.org.

INDEX

Picture Credits

ABOUT THE AUTHOR

Kim K. Zach earned a bachelor's degree in English and a master's degree in education technology. She has taught English in grades 7–12 for twenty-three years. She is the author of numerous magazine articles, two books, and a play. She is a lifelong resident of Nebraska, where she lives with her husband and two children.